Quaich

An Anthology
of Translation
in Scotland Today

Edited by

Madeleine Campbell
Georgina Collins
Anikó Szilágyi

evertype

2014

Published by Evertype, Cnoc Sceichín, Leac an Anfa, Cathair na Mart, Co. Mhaigh Eo, Éire. *www.evertype.com.*

A catalogue record for this book is available from the British Library.

ISBN-10 1-78201-069-6
ISBN-13 978-1-78201-069-2

Typeset in Baskerville by Michael Everson.

Cover: Michael Everson.
Cover photograph © 2014 by Robin Wood of a 3½-inch wooden quaich made by him in Hope Valley, Derbyshire. www.robin-wood.co.uk.
Inside Photographs © 2014 by Monique Lara-Lise Campbell, www.moniquelaralisephotography.com.

Printed by LightningSource.

Table of Contents

Foreword

"Bless thee, Bottom! bless thee! thou art translated."

In *A Midsummer Night's Dream*, the sight of Bottom with his donkey's head provokes Quince to describe him as "translated". The truth is that, when it comes to translating from one language to another, it is entirely possible to end up with the flat-pack assembled back-to-front, if not quite a human with the head of a donkey.

The etymology of "translate" takes us to Latin *transfere*, literally "transferred", but one cannot, for instance, transfer a poem from Gaelic to English as though it were a container being moved from a ship to a lorry. Perhaps that simile is unfair to English, but it does convey a sense of the potential loss of a beautiful economy of concept and sound that Old Gaelic in particular exploits.

Speech is a specialization of music. We learn it from its sounds, and that learning starts even in the womb. Pitch; rhythm; the distribution of rhyme, assonance and alliteration; line, sentence, stanza, paragraph and chapter lengths: they all are part of the flow of sound, be it spoken in the head or out loud. But in the sophisticated extensions of meaning – the semantic content with all its niceties, precisions and ambiguities – sound can be taken for granted, even ignored, and beauty sacrificed. Not so in this book. Read it slowly. It has particular strengths, not just in the variety of languages translated, but the fact that they are sometimes translated into more than one language on the same page, and not always in the one direction.

The variety is impressive. The languages of Scotland are represented here by Gaelic, Scots, English, and Shetlandic, to list them broadly in the order in which they came to be spoken in Scotland.

The latter three are closely enough related to be relatively accessible throughout the English-speaking world. They, along with French, Icelandic, Russian, Swiss German, Italian and Greek, are Indo-European languages and share many common elements.

Gaelic is also an Indo-European language, but it belongs in a group with fundamental differences from most European languages. In particular, Gaelic is a VSO (Verb-Subject-Object) language, giving precedence to the action over the actor. To some, it can seem almost as "foreign" as the non-Indo-European languages represented here: Finnish and Māori. But whatever its classification, every language carries with it its own sound world and presents its own preconditions to the expression of thought. Such topics are taken up in the four introductory essays, which give a splendid depth of perspective to the whole.

The idea that language can determine how one thinks has been much criticized – almost discarded. However, if one presents the idea a little differently – by stating that language determines how one's thought is perceived – then a book such as this provides eloquent support for the statement, just as Lorimer's outstanding translation of the New Testament into Scots provides a radically fresh perception of Christ and the apostles. The corollary is that any bard, makar or writer, conscious of how expression operates on others, is going to mould those expressions within the possibilities of the chosen language – albeit often stretching them to the limits. In translation, those limits are stretched beyond linguistic boundaries and challenge the preconditions that necessarily attach to each individual language.

So it is that the fascination with what follows here goes beyond literary skill and penetrates the world of philosophy. This book plays with thought and beauty, using different languages as the musical instruments upon which the writers perform.

John Purser
April 2014

Introduction:
How Scotland Translates

Madeleine Campbell and Anikó Szilágyi

This collection of essays and translations has been compiled to sample and reflect on contemporary Scotland's rich tradition of literary translation. The title is symbolic of how the anthology is to be read: as an offering, an act of kindness, an opportunity to gain insight into other cultures. "Quaich" is a term derived from the Scottish Gaelic word *cuach*, and it refers to a traditional two-handled drinking cup, usually made of wood or metal. The quaich has a special place in Scottish history; it was used to offer guests a cup of welcome, and the craft of quaich-making was held in high regard. Translation can sometimes be seen as an unfriendly, invasive, even treacherous, act, but this volume aims to celebrate what is good about literary translation, its power to bring together, rather than to separate. All the texts contained here have a vital connection to Scotland through their authors or translators, languages or themes. They are as diverse as Scotland is today, itself a plurality of languages and peoples. The publication of such a volume is timely, not just because in the lead-up to the Scottish independence referendum in 2014 the concepts of Scotland and Scottishness are the subject of renewed debate, but also because of the increased popularity of translation in today's international literary landscape. Translators have an important part to play in this changing context, and their contribution to this anthology is foregrounded to reflect their role as catalysts in the alchemy of cultural transfer, from selection of source material to collaboration with authors.

Literary Translation Now

The twenty-first century has seen the interest in literary translation grow throughout the English-speaking world, accompanied by developments in the study of translated literature. This process did not just begin in the year 2000, of course. In the 1980s the discipline of Translation Studies took what is now referred to as "the cultural turn", and scholars started to pay more attention to translation in its social and historical context. The expansion of the discipline continued into the next decade: in *Constructing Cultures* (1998), Susan Bassnett called Translation Studies "one of the fastest-growing interfields of the 1990s." The twenty-first century has brought about new changes in the way translated texts are produced, published and read, as well as shifts in the discussions surrounding translation. For example, the focus of Translation Studies has expanded to encompass lesser-spoken languages, some of which are represented in this volume. The recent foregrounding of translation is noticeable in countries like the United Kingdom and the United States in particular, but it is also reflected in broader initiatives, some Europe-wide, others reaching into geographical and cultural areas we often define in opposition to "the West". It would be impossible to list every recent development in the areas of literary translation and Translation Studies, therefore what follows is a brief and necessarily selective overview of new translation-related initiatives.

In the UK, well-established institutions like English PEN and the British Centre for Literary Translation have been joined by new organizations to continue raising the profile of translated literature nationwide and beyond. A case in point is Literature Across Frontiers (LAF), an organization founded in Wales in 2001 to promote cross-cultural conversation through literature in Europe, but which has since extended its activities to parts of Asia. LAF publishes *Transcript*, a unique, trilingual, online journal that makes European literature freely accessible in English, French and German. In the same year that LAF was born, Arts Council England decided to resurrect, after a five-year hiatus, the Independent Foreign Fiction Prize, which celebrates the best of contemporary prose fiction translated into English and published in the UK. The significance of this prize is manifold, but it is worth mentioning that the award is split equally between writer and translator, an important acknowledgement of the creative collaboration that translated works represent. Outstanding poetry translations are acknowledged, among others, by the annual Stephen Spender Prize, established in 2004. English PEN also support literary translation financially, but slightly differently. Their "Writers in Translation" programme was launched in 2005 to help publishers to promote translated literature, and since 2012 they also offer grants directly to translators through their "PEN Translates!" initiative. Another remarkable example of efforts to bring together contemporary pieces of world literature for the enjoyment of all is the European Literature Nights 2012-2014 project. Each year people gather together on the designated night in various European cities, from Lisbon to Malmö, to listen to public readings of literary works from other countries. Like access to *Transcript*, admission to these public readings is free.

The role of translation and translations is changing in the cultural landscape of the United States, too. Edwin Gentzler has referred to the recent proliferation of translated literature on the American market as "the translation turn in creative writing," a phrase that echoes the "cultural turn" in Translation Studies as well as the "translation turn" in cultural studies that Bassnett called for in 1998. The launch of the Three Percent website by the University of Rochester in 2007 can be considered a landmark in the history of translation in the US. The creation of this website was inspired by the claim that "only about 3% of all books published in the United States are works in translation." This statement, although problematic and possibly imprecise due to the difficulties of data collection, has become a cliché in the discourse surrounding translation, so much so that it gave its name to LAF's 2013 research report on the state of literary translation in the United Kingdom and Ireland. Although the phrase appears in the title of the report with a question mark ('Three Percent?') and the report concludes that the figure in Britain is actually "consistently greater than 4%", there is no doubt that the Three Percent website has been successful in highlighting the marginalized position of translated fiction in the

Anglophone world. Furthermore, in 2008 the website launched its own literary prize, the Best Translated Book Awards, which are very similar to the British Independent Prize for Foreign Fiction, although they include an award for poetry translations.

In the second half of the twentieth century, traditions outside of Western thinking came into the foreground of cultural studies in general, and of the study of translation in particular. As Brian James Baer writes in "Cultures of Translation" (2007), "the exploration of alternative, non-Western traditions – largely Asian but recently African, as well – has become increasingly visible in recent years as a reaction to hegemonic Western modes of translation and the general eurocentrism of contemporary Translation Studies." The *Girona Manifesto on Linguistic Rights*, based on PEN's 1996 *Universal Declaration of Linguistic Rights* and ratified at PEN's 77th Congress in 2011, is a crucial recognition of the *universal* need for linguistic diversity in the new millennium, and is aimed at securing the rights of linguistic communities worldwide.

In practical terms, the availability in English of texts from across the globe has been greatly facilitated by a number of new online initiatives, such as Words Without Borders, founded in 2003. "Our publications and programs open doors for readers of English around the world to the multiplicity of viewpoints, richness of experience, and literary perspective on world events offered by writers in other languages," their manifesto reads. Words Without Borders have published several print anthologies, including *Literature from the "Axis of Evil": Writing from Iran, Iraq, North Korea, and Other Enemy Nations* (2007), and *Tablet and Pen: Literary Landscapes of the Middle East* (2011). Another fascinating new translation project is *Asymptote*, a journal international not only in its scope but in its editorial board: "*Asymptote* is everywhere and nowhere. Our founder lives in Taipei, Taiwan, [but] the 30+ members of *Asymptote*'s team hail from all over the globe." The journal's quarterly issues focus on literature translated into English, and, similarly to many other initiatives mentioned here, online access to them is completely free. Making literature available in the world's most widely used *lingua franca* is no doubt the best way to reach the widest possible readership, although this does not detract from the importance of translation into lesser-spoken languages. Accordingly, any exploration of literary translation in Scotland must go beyond an examination of translation into English alone.

Translation and Scotland in the Twenty-First Century

Scotland has been a multilingual, multicultural country for many centuries, but issues of language and translation have become increasingly prominent in recent years, in both literary and non-literary contexts. This interest is reflected in a range of areas from policy-making to grassroots initiatives. The fight to revive Scottish Gaelic gathered momentum with the Gaelic Language (Scotland) Act in 2005, which reinstated Gaelic as an official language of Scotland, opening up new horizons in translation between Gaelic and English. Another recent top-down initiative focusing on translation was established by the UK's biggest funding body for the Arts, the Arts and Humanities Research Council (AHRC), whose key research theme "Translating Cultures" has enhanced the analysis of translation and cultural transfer, not only by translators and Translation Studies scholars, but by researchers working in a range of fields across the Arts and Social Sciences. According to the AHRC, "in a world increasingly characterized by transnational and globalized connections, the need for understanding and communication between and across diverse cultures is stronger than ever."

It is in response to this need that a team of researchers at the University of Glasgow, led by Professor Alison Phipps, were awarded a major grant in 2013 to investigate problems of language related to migration. Their project, called "Researching Multilingually at the Borders of the Body, Language, Law and the State", draws on Professor Phipps and her colleagues' work through the Glasgow Refugee Asylum and Migration Network (GRAMNet). "Researching Multilingually" brings together academics from the UK, Netherlands, Bulgaria, Arizona and Gaza and artists from Pan African Arts Scotland in order to better understand and represent what gets "lost in translation" in interactions between refugees and asylum seekers and the state. The assumption underlying this type of research is that translation is not a neutral activity, and researching it often requires genuine engagement with social problems. The project is a collaboration between scholars and a variety of non-academic partners that include Oxfam, the Ethnic Minorities Law Centre, Creative Scotland and the Scottish Refugee Council, and serves as a powerful reminder of how effective the study of translation can be when theory and practice come together.

Scottish universities are playing an important role in both encouraging the study of translation and responding to the increased need for translator and interpreter training. In addition to more established Translation Studies programmes, such as those of Heriot-Watt University and the University of Edinburgh, the Universities of Stirling and Glasgow have recently launched their own postgraduate courses (in 2010 and 2012, respectively). Alongside teaching and training, these and other universities facilitate networking for Translation Studies scholars through a series of translation-themed academic events. These include the upcoming postgraduate conference at Glasgow, "Alternatives: Translation and the (Anti-)Canon", co-organized with St Andrews and the British Comparative Literature Association with the support of Scottish PEN, and the "Translation Training Symposium in Your Subject in the Digital Age for Non-Linguists", to take place at Stirling in the summer of 2014. The work of Scottish PEN is socially engaged, like much of current academic research on translation, but with a strong emphasis on literary translation. Scottish PEN's Translation and Minority Languages group has focused in recent years on encouraging writing in Gaelic and Scots, and on workshops bringing together Scottish and overseas writers based in Scotland who have translated each other's work. This type of cross-cultural collaboration is also something that many of the *Quaich* contributors make use of: Jennifer Williams's rendition of Haris Psarras's poems is one example, and Christine De Luca and Riina Katajavouri have also translated each other's works.

Among all the translation activities taking place in Scotland today, literary translation stands out in two senses. Firstly, Scotland is becoming increasingly self-aware as an important centre for artistic production on the international literary scene. Edinburgh had the honour of becoming the first UNESCO City of Literature in 2004, a title it now shares with Melbourne, Iowa City, Dublin, Reykjavík, Norwich and Kraków. Edinburgh's City of Literature Trust was founded to actively promote Scottish literature both at home and abroad, and as part of its international outreach programme, the organization represented Scotland as the Guest Country at the 2009 Kolkata Book Fair. The Association for Scottish Literary Studies, which calls itself "Scottish Literature's New International Voice", is also instrumental in the marketing of Scottish literature internationally, and their website conveniently lists the upcoming Scottish literary and linguistic conferences worldwide. Scotland is also doing well at keeping track of how its literature is "exported" to other countries, in spite of the difficulties of defining what constitutes Scottish literature. The Bibliography of Scottish Literature in Translation (BOSLIT), a freely accessible online database run jointly by the University of Edinburgh and the National Library of Scotland, is an invaluable research tool. BOSLIT is relatively up-to-date and, unlike most translation databases, enables searches of translations from Scotland as a whole, rather than from specific languages spoken in the country. Dennis Smith demonstrates the uses of BOSLIT in the present volume in his essay on the communication of ideas of modernity in Asia through translations of Scottish writing.

Secondly, translation into or between Scotland's languages occupies a prominent position in the vibrant Scottish literary scene. The most spectacular manifestation of this interest in world literature is no doubt the Edinburgh International Book Festival, one of the world's largest book festivals, which welcomes over 800 writers, poets, musicians and thinkers every year from all over the world, and which celebrated its thirtieth birthday last year. 2013 was significant for the Festival for other reasons, too: it saw the return of the Edinburgh World Writers' Conference to the city after its twelve-month journey visiting fifteen different countries, and it featured a series of events dedicated specifically to literary translation. These included "Translation Duels", where two translators presented and compared their versions of the same text, an all-day translation workshop led by Ros Schwartz, and a discussion of Adam Thirlwell's project "Multiples" with translator Daniel Hahn and novelists John

Banville and Nadeem Aslam. The events attracted unexpectedly large audiences, and many of them sold out.

Scotland is also home to the international poetry festival, StAnza, which takes place annually in St Andrews, and showcases the best of contemporary Scottish writing as well as poetry from over 40 countries worldwide. In 2010, StAnza introduced a new regular feature, Border Crossings, where poets from different countries writing in different languages share a platform. Readings are in the poets' native tongues as well as in English translation. In 2013, Anna Crowe introduced her new set of translations in *Six Catalan Poets*, part of Arc's *New Voices from Europe* series. Crowe had previously co-translated Catalan poems with Christoper Whyte, which were published in *Light Off Water* in 2007. In 2014, StAnza also featured a public discussion on translation with poets Menna Elfyn (Welsh), Tomica Bajsić (Croatian), Arjen Duinker (Dutch), and Marco Fazzini (Italian). In addition to its international literary festivals, as of April 2013 Scotland has its own journal dedicated solely to the translation of poetry, *Scottish Poetry in Translation*. The Glasgow-based journal accepts submissions in any of Scotland's languages, and the first issue featured the works of students alongside pieces by established poets and translators, including Aonghas MacNeacail, Alan Riach and John Purser. As the journal's title suggest, translation is integral to this new project, as it is to all of the initiatives mentioned above. However, translation is present even when it doesn't take centre stage: the Scottish Writers' Centre runs a Scots-English and a Gaelic Writing Group, which have no explicit translation component, but exemplify what it means to live and write multilingually in Scotland today. Of course, Scotland's engagement with translation is not a new phenomenon, and the history of Scottish literature cannot be discussed independently of the history of Scottish literary translation.

"Our Ane Language"

Translation has formed an integral part of the Scottish literary tradition for a very long time. Centuries before Sir Walter Scott decided to collect and preserve the ballads in the tongue of the borders – which in turn represented an ancient oral and musical tradition – another Scot set out to translate Virgil's *Aeneid* while "keeping nae southern, but our ane language". The Middle Scots *Eneados*, written in 1513, was first published in 1553 (the c.1525 Cambridge manuscript version was reprinted in 1839 by the Bannatyne club, founded by Sir Walter Scott). Its author, Gavin Douglas, clergyman and poet, prefaced *Eneados* with a remarkably modern outlook on translation:

> Weel at ae blenk slee poetry nocht taen is
> And yet, forsooth, I set my busy pain
> As that I should, to mak it braid and plain,
> Keeping nae southern, but our ane language,
> And speaks as I learnit when I was a page.
> Nor yet sae clean all southern I refuse,
> But some word I pronounce as neighbour does,
> Like as in Latin been Greek terms sum,
> So me behovit whilom (or then be dumb)
> Some bastard Latin, French or English use
> Where scant were Scots I had nae other choice.

The reader will be more struck by the consonance between the language of Douglas' poem and the songs collected in Sir Walter Scott's *Minstrelsy of the Scottish Border*, published in 1802-1803, or Robert Burns' Ayrshire *Poems, Chiefly in the Scottish Dialect* – whose first Kilmarnock edition, dated 1786, is separated from the Douglas manuscript by over two centuries, not to mention the geographical spread of these texts. Further, a glance at the Scots translations featured in *Quaich* suggests a remarkable continuity in the cadence, tonality and diction of the idiom to this day. Stewart Alexander Sanderson, poet and editor of *Scottish Poetry in Translation*, credits Douglas, who was educated at the University of St Andrews, with setting the standard for modern translation into Scots: "This [introductory poem] quite literally sets out Douglas' twin intentions: to write in the vernacular tongue and through translation into it to enlarge its range and vocabulary."

Yet the Lallans or Lowland Scots we can trace back to Douglas and his contemporaries forms but one geo-historicist trope in the complex web of dialects and languages that make up the tongues from which Scotland's expression, past and present, is spun: "We grow up in a web of language to which feelings are attached", as Iain Crichton Smith (or Iain Mac a'Ghobhainn) once observed. And while, according to Wilson McLeod, "modern perceptions of relations in the Gaelic world can often be clouded by nostalgia or nationalism," the same could be said of Lowland Scots and its ideological appropriation by Hugh MacDiarmid and the Renaissance poets in the early twentieth century. Thomas Owen Clancy's illuminating 1998 *The Triumph Tree*, which brings together poems from Latin, Welsh, Gaelic, Anglo Saxon and Norse in English translation, is a welcome illustration of the early mix of languages that prevailed between the sixth century CE and the fourteenth century in the region we now call Scotland. *The Triumph Tree*, together with Clancy's *Iona: The Earliest Poetry of a Celtic Monastery*, reminds us that Gaelic was the language of early "Goidelic" Christianity. *Quaich* celebrates this early connection with Brian Johnstone's poem sequence on Celtic saints, *Cothan/Reliquary*, translated into Gaelic by Christopher Whyte (Crìsdean MacIlleBhàin).

Silke Stroh's 2011 analysis of the socio-cultural forces that shaped Scottish Gaelic poetry, entitled *Uneasy Subjects*, provides a fascinating account of how Gaelic, Scottish and British identities later came to be drawn along linguistic lines. What we have come to refer to as Scotland's polyglot status has been the case "from the earliest times", as John Corbett relates in his lucid exposé on literary translation into Scots (1999). He charts the arrival of the "Scoti", who crossed over from Ireland in to Argyll or *Dàl Riata* in the fifth century CE, speaking an ancient version of today's Scottish Gaelic, while to the South a Brythonic Celtic related to Welsh was the dominant language, as was Pictish to the North. According to Stroh, by the eighth century, though it was the language of the royal court, "the Gaelic language co-existed with Pictish, Cumbrian, Norse and Anglo-Saxon". By the tenth century it was spoken by much of the Scottish population, "reaching its maximum currency during the eleventh and early twelfth century". Stroh observes that it wasn't until the fourteenth century that a "Highland Line" distinction was made between the "gaelophone and anglophone populace" and the terms "Highlands" and "Lowlands" started to be recorded. Clancy, however, notes earlier signs of this divide in *Fergus of Galloway*, composed in Old French in the early thirteenth century, and even in the twelfth-century *The Song on the Death of Somerled*, an account of the 1164 battle of Renfrew.

Noting that French arrived at the court of Gaelic King Malcolm III after the Norman Conquest, Corbett relates that by the twelfth century, the main languages in Lowland Scotland were Gaelic, English and French, together with Latin and some Norse. At the risk of simplifying, Latin and French tended to be the languages of religious and legal officialdom, but they gave way to "Inglis" in the Lowlands of medieval Scotland, "a distinctive variety of northern English" later known as "Scots", and from the fourteenth to the seventeenth century this came close to a "national language". While Latin remained the language of academic discourse well into the seventeenth century, Inglis gradually infiltrated all genres. Initially through the agency of translating from the incumbent languages of authority, its development was led principally in the domain of literature through the translation and adaptation of French romances, from which Inglis borrowed vocabulary to extend its register. Centuries later the legacy of the Auld Alliance, though put to bed politically when Scotland signed the Union with England Act in 1707, continues to inspire Scotland's poets past and present. Richie McCaffery's essay in this volume, for example, reviews creative approaches of post-war second wave poets of the Scottish Literary Renaissance, Tom Scott, William J. Tait and Norman Cameron, in their versions of fifteenth-century French poet François Villon.

During the High Middle Ages, Gaelic expanded eastward, then "receded west then north", continues Corbett. It was to travel as far as Caithness and span a region now commonly referred to as the Highlands and Islands of Scotland (though it didn't reach Orkney and Shetland). McLeod describes the period of "the 'Lordship of the Isles', the dominant political force in Gaelic Scotland from *c.*1150 to *c.*1550 [...], as *Linn an Àigh*, the age of joy (or prosperity)", though scholars lament that there are few extant literary traces of the golden age of Gaelic Scotland, in contrast with the Bardic Poetry of Gaelic Ireland.

Orkney and Shetland had been colonized by Scandinavians in the ninth century and according to Clancy, Old Norse extended for some time the length of the West Coast of Scotland. Noting that for Gaelic and Norse, the cultural centres were Ireland and Scandinavia, criteria for the selection of poetry which could be attributed to Scotland in *The Triumph Tree* had to be based on the origins or place of residence of poets rather than genre or style, though there were exceptions. These ancient linguistic ties and their continuing relevance are represented in *Quaich* through contemporary poets Aðalsteinn Ásberg Sigurðsson (Iceland) and Thor Sørheim (Norway). Their verse is translated into Shetlandic by poet Christine De Luca, who also offers Shetlandic versions of poems by Riina Katajavuori (Finland), while Donald Adamson translates Eeva Kilpi, also from Finland, into English.

From Salt Herring to *Sovpoems*

Today in Scotland the Gaelic language is mainly spoken in the Inner and Outer Hebrides as well as Argyll and Bute. Although, as noted earlier, the status of the language has gained cultural recognition since the Gaelic Language (Scotland) Act 2005, only some 58,000 could speak Gaelic in 2011, a number that dwindled from the c. 289,298 who spoke Gaelic as their first and main language in 1755, the date of the first census of Scotland. This linguistic marginalization is reflected in Kevin MacNeil's characterization of the "modern" poets from the Scottish Islands assembled in his 2011 *These Islands We Sing* as the "the sidelined of the sidelined."

In contrast, according to the 2011 Scotland Census, some 1.5 million people spoke Scots "regularly". This disparity is reflected in the corpus of Scottish literary translation, where the predominant direction of translation, other than into English, is into Lowland Scots, urban or synthetic, rather than Gaelic. When considering the value or relevance of a lesser-spoken language, however, statistics on numbers of speakers or texts hold little sway. The heritage of the Gaelic language is ubiquitous in the Scottish cultural landscape, in its place names, loanwords, myths and legends. Though not all possess an understanding of Gaelic, its melodic quality, rich singing traditions and poetry, whether classical or contemporary, form part of this nation's cultural history from the Early Middle Ages, and this is reflected in a strong will to nourish and nurture the language. Contemporary challenges and controversies associated with the role and perception of Gaelic in translation are discussed in McLeod's essay in this volume.

When the aforementioned Crichton Smith's Gaelic-speaking protagonist first went to school in *Thoughts of Murdo*, he was confronted with the English language in the form of "a starved looking very tall thin woman". The eponymous Murdo turned half-red, half-black: "There was a smell of salt herring from the black half, and a smell of bacon from the other half." He used his right hand to write in Gaelic and his left to write in English, though "later these physical processes were reversed." The physical symptoms were so intense that "in periods of stress he was completely immobilised, i.e he could not write at all." Although Crichton Smith refers here to the physical act of writing, there is a clear allusion to the psychological, cultural and literary implications for the writer (and hence the translator) of straddling several cultures, or speaking two or more languages.

In his review of Linda MacDonald-Lewis' conversations with Alan Riach and Alexander Moffat in *Arts of Resistance: Poets, Portraits and Landscapes of Modern Scotland* (2009), Neal Ascherson reminds us that Crichton Smith was "surely one of the most marvellous of Scottish poets". He was also a consummate storyteller of ferocious humour, and turned the early trauma of enforced bilingualism to considerable creative advantage. He was equally at home in "Scotland's three languages," and could slip seamlessly between English, Lowland Scots, and Gaelic, sometimes in the same poem, as in "A Bilingual Poem By Murdo (With Analysis)". That he calls this a bilingual, rather than trilingual, poem betrays the widespread perception in Scotland that people generally "don't really think of Scots as a language – it's more just a way of speaking", an opinion held by 64% of those interviewed in the Scottish Government's report on Public Attitudes to the Scots Language in 2010.

But translation from Gaelic was also important to Crichton Smith, and in 1971 his English versions of the *Dàin do Eimhir* (*Poems to Eimhir*) brought the Hebridean Gaelic poet Sorley MacLean (Somhairle MacGill-Eain) to a wider audience. Maclean had previously been translated into Scots by Robert Garioch, Sidney Goodsir Smith, and Douglas Young; and J. Derrick McClure "owerset" him in 2011, commenting that if Scots can offer a "hameilt tung tae sing wi" to poets from Homer to Akhmatova, "an mony anither forbye, it can bode a wordie welcome tae Sorley MacLean". Although MacLean wrote in Gaelic, he provided his own cribs in English, and also translated Gaelic poems for Hugh MacDiarmid's 1940 anthology *The Golden Treasury of Scottish Verse*, while Hugh MacDiarmid, who first wrote in Scots Lallans, gradually turned to English as his language of expression.

Following the Scottish Renaissance led by MacDiarmid and subsequently taken up by the post-war poets, translation into Scots continued to be a source of inspiration and a medium against which to test the possibilities of the language in a modern context. When researching the "second generation Renaissance poets (c. 1940-1981)", Sanderson noted that "clearly, to translate poetry into a minor, frequently unrecognized language is to make a risky and emphatically political statement about the role and nature of language in the modern world." His statement on Garioch and Goodsir Smith's translations of French Modernist poetry probably still stands for much translation into Scots today: "They test the possibilities of a non-official, synthetic language, which is both oral and historicist in its vocabulary and grammar; medieval and modern experienced not as a smooth chronological progression but two extremes thrust together in the act of translation."

The late twentieth century saw a continued revival of translation into Scots, notably through Edwin Morgan's prolific verse trans-lations, which spanned most of his writing life, starting with his celebrated 1961 *Sovpoems* featuring the great Russian poets Boris Pasternak, Marina Tsvetayeva, and Vladimir Mayakovski. James McGonigal relates how Morgan's consuming interest in translation, with his "defiantly un-parochial internationalist leanings," initially alienated established Scottish poets. Though he enlisted Glaswegian Scots to render Edmond Rostand's *Cyrano de Bergerac: A New Verse Translation* (1992), Morgan wasn't averse to a purely English medium when he judged it appropriate for the source text. In August 1983 he wrote of his earlier adaptation of the anonymous fifteenth-century French farce *Master Peter Pathelin*, in a letter to Carl Heap, director of the Medieval Players: "The English version sits very loosely to the text, has continuous omissions, dilutes the luxurious religious oaths, and bowdlerizes the whole vocabulary, especially that of bodily functions. I have restored the outspokenness and I hope the pungency." For the set piece he refers to as the "feast of languages", he tells us in his Translator's Note that he substituted "Scots, German, Italian, Russian, and Latin' for the farce's "seven garbled tongues", namely "Limousin, Picardy, Flemish, Norman, Breton, Lorrainese and Latin". Throughout Morgan's writing life, translation proved a means of both expanding his own expression and pushing at national boundaries beyond the restrictions of a potentially narrow, inward-looking gaze.

Soon *an* Sense?

Translation continues to hold the power to help our poets rediscover their language. Liz Lochhead, whom Margery Palmer McCulloch considers the successor of Edwin Morgan, following Hugh MacDiarmid, as Scotland's Makar, adapted Molière's *Tartuffe* by the poolside on a trip to California. In an interview with *The Herald* on 3 January 2006 she commented: "Tartuffe speaks theatre. It gave me the language for *Mary Queen Of Scots Got Her Head Chopped Off*. It gave me Scots. I didn't know I had it in me." And Corbett tells us in his review of the essays edited by Bill Finlay in *Frae Ither Tongues* (2004) that

> there is a strong feeling, typical of Scots translators [...], that the pressure of adapting a classic source text results in an extended spoken medium that promises to establish a norm for written Scots. This promise is never satisfied because each translation (however aesthetically pleasing) is too idiosyncratic to serve as a model for general usage. As [Brian] Holton argues, the act of translating is one of endless reinvention of one's own language – a process peculiarly visible in many contemporary Scots translations.

To this day, regional diversity has continued to reflect the socio-historical conditions that shape the nation's many voices and, alongside English, contemporary writing ranges widely from the urban vernaculars or demotics of Glasgow, to those of Edinburgh, Dundee or Aberdeen, from "synthetic" Lallans to Shetlandic, from traditional Doric to varieties of Scottish Gaelic. Scotland's feelings are thus woven of many tongues, and translation into or out of these has a role to play in articulating the nexus of interrelations that make up what we have come to call Scottish literature.

The best of contemporary Scots translation has kept up with this multi-ethnic horizon as do, for example twin brothers Brian and Harvey Holton's 2005 translations of the dissident Chinese poet Yang Liang *Whaur The Deep Sea Devauls*. In Harvey Holton's "Sixteeners", the poem entitled "STILL" achieves a remarkable modernity in the subtle evocation of the source poem's lexical and auditory landscape without compromising the authenticity of the Scots:

> still is a palindrome   cawsey fuu o leein bairns
> still is oan the thin edge o the lotus-leaf o the yird
> clood nibbling a wee eraser thoomb
> Different kinds o still   there's still
> a cocoon   cooryin a lover's reek like cooryin doun wi
>   a piano solo
> dauncin   wame in daith thraws in the daunce-steps
> still listenin tae the telegram's soond French-neckin the past
>   intae a
> private maitter
> [...]

As John Purser suggests in his Foreword to *Quaich*, these tongues are to be heard like different instruments. In today's voices, whether Gaelic or demotic Scots, it is perhaps even more true to say that "*It's soon, no' sense, that faddoms the herts o'men*" (MacDiarmid, "Gairmscoile", 1926, author's italics). Yet in this manifesto poem, MacDiarmid also called for the "*rouch auld Scots I ken*" with a dubious incantation to "the spirit o' the race", a concept that reflects the dangerously fascist *zeitgeist* of his time but one which is much out of place in today's multi-ethnic Scotland. Returning to the 2011 Scotland Census, we find that after English the ten most widely used languages were, in descending order, Scots, Gaelic, Polish, Urdu, Punjabi, Chinese, French, British Sign Language, German and Spanish, all with over 10,000 speakers (at 54,000, there are nearly as many Polish as Gaelic speakers in Scotland today). Many of these languages are represented in this volume, and, as the reader will discover, their sound and sense are rich and varied.

In this volume, Colin Donati's Scots version of a passage from Fyodor Dostoevsky's *Crime and Punishment* translates a late nineteenth century urban setting that wouldn't be out of place in Morgan's Glasgow:

> *Sanct Petersburg in the swaltry simmer o 1865. The ex-student Raskolnikov, on the mornin efter cairryin oot his premeditated murder o a local pawnwife, is waukent in bumbazement in his attic lodgins – the fouty chaumer he canna afford to pey the rent on – by the unexpectit delivery o a summons to cry in at the local bureau o the polis for his side o the city. Forbye his confusion, and teeterin wi the onset o a fever, the young murderer walks oot in the switherin city heat to obey the fearfu summons....*

A C Clarke, Sarah Paterson, and Christine DeLuca present poems twice translated, with the source texts appearing alongside both an English and a regional Scots translation. The sad death last year of the Irish Nobel laureate poet Seamus Heaney, and the many public readings and tributes in homage to him, have reminded us once again of the strong cultural ties that link Ireland and Scotland, and Morna Fleming celebrates Heaney's contribution to Scottish poetry in his rewriting of Robert Henryson's *Testament of Cresseid*.

These and other texts selected for *Quaich* either illustrate or serve to establish links between diverse linguistic communities living in Scotland today. Sarah Paterson's translations from Māori in New Zealand, traditionally a popular emigration destination, reflect her experience in recent decades of the increased recognition and nurture of the Māori language and reverse the diaspora, linguistically at least, by bringing something of Māori culture into Scots. Immigration and multiculturalism are also prominent issues in Monica Cantieni's *The Encyclopaedia of Good Reasons*, translated from Swiss German into English by Donal McLaughlin, in an extract that explores topical issues of "foreignness", politics and referendums. Donald Adamson's translation from "Voices from an Old People's Home" by Eeva Kilpi, Chair of Finnish PEN and featured writer of Scottish PEN, remind us that "the need for understanding and communication between and across diverse cultures" refers not just to the cultures of different countries but to the voices of different generations, too.

Is diversity, then, both in the languages and dialects of Scotland and in their interplay with other languages, what defines Scottish culture? Is Alan Riach right in claiming that "our distinction" is "in a sense of our own multiplicity in languages, voices, geographies"? If so, *Quaich* contributes a contemporary anthology to this vision of Scotland through new translations of texts from a spirited kaleidoscope of "languages, voices, geographies" – and epochs. Just as this introduction could only hint at the tangled web of emerging and established authors, poets and translators who have come to shape how Scotland translates, this eclectic assemblage hints at, without being comprehensive, fresh and fluid literary currents in a hybrid cultural context. The comments and insights cited here attest to the vibrant, even urgent, sense that translation, whether version or theme, continues to offer perennial opportunities for inventiveness and renewal in contemporary Scotland.

Further Reading

Bassnett, Susan, and André Lefevere. *Constructing Cultures*. Clevedon: Multilingual Matters, 1998.

Corbett, John. *Language and Scottish Literature*. Edinburgh: Edinburgh University Press, 1997.

—. *Topics in Translation 14: Written in the Language of the Scottish Nation: A History of Translation into Scots*. Clevedon: Multilingual Matters, 1999.

Fazzini, Marco. *Crossings: Essays on Contemporary Scottish Literature and Hybridity*. Venezia: Supernova Edizioni, 2000.

—. *Topics in Translation 24: Frae Ither Tongues: Essays on Modern Translations into Scots*. Ed. Bill Findlay. Clevedon: Multilingual Matters, 2004.

McCulloch, Margery Palmer. "From MacDiarmid and Morgan to Lochhead and Kay: Bards, Radicals, and the Place of Europe in Modern Scottish Poetry". In *Scotland in Europe, Europe in Scotland*. Eds. Aniela Korzeniowska and Izabela Szymańska, 168-181. Semper: Warszawa, 2013.

McLeod, Wilson. *Divided Gaels: Gaelic Cultural Identities in Scotland and Ireland 1200-1650*. Oxford University Press: Oxford/New York, 2004.

Riach, Alan, Alexander Moffat and Linda MacDonald-Lewis. *Arts of Resistance: Poets, Portraits and Landscapes of Modern Scotland*. Luath Press: Edinburgh, 2009.

Sanderson, Stewart Alexander. "'The Moon and the Pathetic Fallacy': Guillaume Apollinaire and the Scottish Renaissance". In *Scotland in Europe, Europe in Scotland*. Eds. Aniela Korzeniowska and Izabela Szymańska, 154-176. Semper: Warszawa, 2013.

Stroh, Silke. *Uneasy Subjects: Postcolonialism and Scottish Gaelic Poetry*. Rodopi: Amsterdam/New York, 2011.

Essays

Translation and Gaelic: Current Challenges and Controversies

Wilson McLeod

The translation of texts from and into Gaelic is inextricably linked to the social and sociolinguistic position of the language and programmatic efforts to strengthen or transform that position. There are now under 60,000 Gaelic speakers in Scotland, only two-thirds of whom can read Gaelic, and there is almost certainly no one who can read Gaelic more easily than English. All Gaelic speakers can speak English, and more and more of them function as English-dominant bilinguals. Literary works and other texts are therefore not created in Gaelic or translated into Gaelic for the benefit of a monoglot population which is unable to access these materials in English. The commissioning and production of translations of literary texts is instead directly linked to language policy and language politics.

As such, literary translation must be understood in the broader context of Gaelic translational activity. As initiatives to sustain and promote Gaelic have gathered pace in recent decades, especially following the enactment of the Gaelic Language (Scotland) Act 2005, an increasing range of official and semi-official documents and publications have been translated into Gaelic by a wide range of public bodies. The policy rationale for these translation initiatives is not always clear; the total proportion of material produced in Gaelic remains small, as these promotion efforts amount to much less than a move towards systematic official bilingualism, such as that practised by the federal government in Canada. The current practice of increasing but sporadic translation of public documents into

3

Gaelic is characteristic of a particular stage in minority language development, in which the authorities take limited steps to accommodate the minority language but stop well short of operating on a genuinely bilingual basis. Production of the Gaelic version is typically outsourced, with the body responsible continuing to function as an essentially monoglot-English organization.

The Scottish Government's Gaelic Language Plan (2010) does articulate a number of criteria to determine whether particular official publications should be made available in Gaelic, though its policy falls well short of the goal proposed by some Gaelic activists, that Gaelic speakers should be enabled to participate in the political and policy process through the medium of Gaelic should they so wish. Controversy has arisen recently, for example, following the Government's refusal to produce a bilingual ballot paper for the 2014 independence referendum.

In contrast to Ireland, where the requirement to produce Irish versions of various official documents is formally embedded in the national language legislation, the cost of producing Gaelic versions of public documents has not attracted much in the way of public controversy. This is surprising given that aggressive attacks on supposedly wasteful spending on Gaelic initiatives (especially bilingual signage) are a mainstay of several Scottish newspapers and writers of letters to their editors. On the other hand, some prominent voices within the Gaelic community, including novelist and poet Aonghas Pàdraig Caimbeul, have complained that the money spent on the translation of official documents would be better spent producing original texts in Gaelic, especially literary texts.

Gaelic versions of public documents are prepared not because Gaelic speakers cannot read the English versions, but "with a view to securing the status of the Gaelic language as an official language of Scotland commanding equal respect to the English language", to quote the ambitious preamble to the Gaelic Language Act. This is an important aspiration, but there is substantial evidence to suggest that few Gaelic speakers actually make use of the Gaelic versions of public documents. One reason for this low rate of take-up is the historic marginalization of Gaelic, which meant that many Gaelic speakers became inured to public services (including education) and public life conducted exclusively in English. Another reason is the accessibility and quality of the Gaelic translations. Typically the Gaelic versions are prepared by outside contractors, under tight time pressure, late in the production process, and there is little quality control (even proofreading by a second pair of Gaelic-literate eyes). There are no training courses or certification structures for Gaelic translators, some kinds of specialist terminology are under-developed, and the range of linguistic resources (dictionaries, thesauruses, databases) remains limited, despite substantial improvements in recent years. As a consequence, many Gaelic versions of public documents contain stylistic infelicities – unnatural, impenetrable, jargonistic expression– as well as grammar and spelling mistakes.

The production of literary texts in Gaelic is also directly linked to the status of the language and to efforts to enhance that status by creating a more vibrant, engaged culture of literacy in Gaelic and a more important role for literature in Gaelic as a site of cultural exchange and debate. The most significant development in Gaelic literature in the twenty-first century has been the rapid growth of prose fiction. More Gaelic novels for adults have been published in the first thirteen years of the twenty-first century than in the nineteenth and twentieth centuries combined. The key factor here is the (sadly now defunct) initiative Ùr-Sgeul, sponsored by the Gaelic Books Council, which led to the publication of more than 30 novels and short story collections beween 2003 and 2013, the most prolific authors being Aonghas Pàdraig Caimbeul, Màrtainn Mac an t-Saoir, Iain Fionnlagh MacLeòid and Norma NicLeòid. Ùr-Sgeul has now been replaced by a new series, Aiteal, published by the Stornoway-based Gaelic publisher Acair, with the first two novels having appeared in 2013.

In sharp contrast to the prevailing practice in relation to Gaelic poetry (discussed below), very little Gaelic fiction has been translated, whether into English or other languages. Norman MacLean has recently published self-translated English versions of three of his comic novels, *Dearest Dacha* (2011, originally *Dacha mo Ghaoil* (2005)), *Tricksters* (2011) (originally *Slaightearan* (2008)) and *Contracts* (2012, originally *Cùmhnantan* (1996)), but his much darker *Keino* (1998)

5

remains in Gaelic only. One volume of short stories, selected from Ùr-Sgeul collections by Màrtainn Mac an t-Saoir and Donnchadh MacGill'Ìosa, has been published in Irish (*Malairt Scéil: Nuascéalaíocht ó Albain* (2006), translated by Antain Mac Lochlainn) and a selection of stories from the multi-author collection *An Claigeann aig Damien Hirst* has been translated into German (*Der Schädel von Damien Hirst*, 2009). The last volume is particularly interesting in that two of the stories were written by German learners of Gaelic, Mìcheal Klevenhaus and Mona Claudia Striewe, and then translated by their authors into German. Klevenhaus has now embarked on a German translation of Aonghas Pàdraig Caimbeul's novel *An Taigh-Samhraidh* (2007); most of Caimbeul's novels remain unavailable in English, but he has recently published both the short story collection *Invisible Islands* (2006) and the novel *Archie and the North Wind* (2010) in English. In 2013, Caimbeul made an innovative move, publishing two versions of the same novel simultaneously in Gaelic and in English (*An Nighean air an Aiseag* and *The Girl on the Ferryboat*). In this case, Caimbeul actually wrote the two texts simultaneously rather than sequentially, so that neither can properly be considered the original or a translation.

Conversely, while few novels or short story collections for adults have been translated into Gaelic, translated works have come to play a very prominent role in the publication of Gaelic children's literature. Relatively few original Gaelic titles for children are produced (or translated from Gaelic into other languages), and a very large proportion of illustrated story books for young children are translated from English, notably the works of Julia Davidson and Axel Scheffler, including *An Gruffalo* (2004). The most prolific translator of children's books into Gaelic is Tormod Caimbeul. Widely considered the pre-eminent novelist in his native language, he brings his keen sense of the phrasing and cadence of traditional Gaelic song to his translations of Davidson's books (among others). In recent years a number of classic works for children have been translated into Gaelic for the first time, notably *Eachdraidh Ealasaid ann an Tìr nan Iongantas (Alice in Wonderland)* (2012), *Am Prionnsa Beag (Le Petit Prince)* (2008), nine books by Beatrix Potter, including *Sgeulachd Pheadair Rabaid* (2008), and two short works by Roald Dahl

(2012). Some material for teenagers has also been translated from Irish, including Éilís Ní Dhuibhne's novel *Úpraid* (originally *Hurlamboc*) (2006) and two short story collections by Ré Ó Laighléis. Taking a longer view, there is little history of imaginative fiction being translated into Gaelic. In interwar Ireland, the newly independent government sponsored an extensive programme of literary translation, commissioning established writers to translate classics from different languages into Irish. There has been a long debate about the value of this initiative, but literary scholar Alan Titley has argued that it played a key role in developing the suppleness of Irish as a modern literary medium, leading eventually to a flowering of original fiction that far outstrips anything seen in Scotland, at least until the arrival of Ùr-Sgeul. In the last third of the twentieth century, a considerable range of short stories were translated from various languages into Gaelic, as in Calum Greum and Donnchadh MacIllIosa's *Thall 's a Bhos* (1991), an anthology that includes translations of stories by José Luis Borges, James Joyce and Isaac Bashevis Singer. Unfortunately, the demise of the literary journal *Gairm* in 2001 has meant the loss of the key outlet for literary translations of this kind – poetry as well as prose.

Translation has been a much more problematic issue in relation to poetry, although (perhaps unsurprisingly) controversy has only arisen in relation to its translation from Gaelic into English. Relatively little poetry has been translated into Gaelic, especially in recent decades, and translation of Gaelic poetry into languages other than English raises few if any hackles.

From the 1970s onwards, more and more collections of Gaelic poetry have tended to be published with *en face* English translations, almost always prepared by the poets themselves. Unlike, for example, Spanish poetry that appears in a bilingual edition for an English-language readership years after its initial appearance in a monolingual Spanish edition, Gaelic poetry rarely has any public existence independent of the bilingual edition. This meant, as I argued in 1998, that:

> The two texts can be understood as two functionally equivalent versions of the same thing, the same ideal

7

'original' – the difference being essentially one of format, like the difference between the compact disc and the vinyl version of 'the same' record. Or the two texts can be seen as two distinct and different compositions, two 'originals' of essentially identical legitimacy and importance, each the fruit of the author's labour, and not necessarily dependent on one another. What no longer seems a realistic interpretation is the most obvious one – that the Gaelic texts are the originals, and their English translations are ancillary and mediated compositions in whose production 'something has been lost'.

One illustration of the difficulties here is the recent decision of the Scottish Qualifications Authority to include a work by the Gaelic poet Somhairle MacGill-Eain among the set texts for the Higher English exam in Scottish secondary schools. The text was MacGill-Eain's English translation of his Gaelic poem "Hallaig", but the pupils would not study the original, and MacGill-Eain's text would be presented as an "English" text belonging to the same category as the other texts studied, all of which were composed in English.

There has been some progress in recent years, however. Although many publishers remain reluctant to publish Gaelic poetry without an accompanying English translation, they have adopted a range of different strategies that arguably serve to highlight the difference between the Gaelic and English texts and signal the subordinate nature of the English translation. It remains debatable whether this is enough to overcome some English readers' sense that the original Gaelic is a "hieroglyph whose oddity [can] be appreciated and dispensed with at a glance", as Christopher Whyte suggested in the introduction to *Dreuchd an Fhigheadair*, a collection described below.

Thus Meg Bateman's collection *Soirbheas/Fair Wind*, published by Polygon in 2007, gives her English translations in italics, whereas her previous collection for Polygon, *Aotromachd agus dàin eile/Lightness and other poems* (1997), used the same Roman font for both the Gaelic and the English texts. Bilingual collections from Acair, including Domhnall MacAmhlaigh's *Deilbh is Faileasan/Images and Reflections* (2008), use a bolder typeface for the Gaelic source texts. Several bilingual editions, including Ruaraidh MacThòmais's *Sùil air fàire/Surveying the horizon* (2007), leave several of the Gaelic poems untranslated, or place the translations at the back of the book, rather than opposite the source texts. Other volumes place the Gaelic texts and not the English translations on the eye-catching right page.

The once almost unquestioned practice of self-translation has come under increasing challenge, and more Gaelic poems are being translated into English by translators other than the authors themselves (a practice that is better established in Ireland). Christopher Whyte's *Bho Leabhar-Latha Maria Malibran/From the Diary of Maria Malibran* (2009) is particularly striking in this regard, with English versions by six different translators, including the author himself, who has been a pungent critic of self-translation.

Whyte was also the architect of a rather different project, *Dreuchd an Fhigheadair – The Weaver's Task: a Gaelic Sampler*, a (very) small book published in 2007 by the Scottish Poetry Library. This involved giving literal English translations of Gaelic poems to Scottish poets with no knowledge of Gaelic and asking them to produce their own "responses" to them (a term Whyte felt more suitable than "translations" or "versions"). The results varied: some retained a considerable connection to the Gaelic source texts, while two of three texts produced by David Kinloch were drastically different, one of them, in response to Aonghas MacNeacail's "dàn", strikingly so.

A little less than a third of the Gaelic poetry collections published between 2004 and 2010 were in a monolingual Gaelic format, and in all only slightly more than half included translations into English. A particularly important all-Gaelic volume is Moray Watson's recent critical edition (2013) of the collected Gaelic poetry of Iain Mac a' Ghobhainn (Iain Crichton Smith). There are no translations for the 331 poems, and the substantial critical apparatus (150 pages in length) is in Gaelic only. The publication of such an important critical edition in Gaelic only is itself part of a noticeable trend in recent years towards the increasing use of Gaelic as a medium for literary scholarship and other academic work (work that will very rarely be available in translation).

For a Gaelic poet to decline publication with *en face* English translations can sometimes represent a political statement. Most of the collections published in Gaelic only tend to be traditional in their

9

subject matter, typically produced by older native speakers of Gaelic living in island communities. A striking exception to the pattern is Niall O'Gallagher's *Beatha Ùr* (2013), with its thematic emphasis on the city of Glasgow, its iconoclastic use of the Italian sonnet form and its eloquent defence of the non-native speaker's entitlement to use Gaelic for creative and emotional exploration.

Translation of Gaelic poetry into languages other than English is less controversial. Since the late 1980s the Dublin publisher Coiscéim has produced a number of Scottish Gaelic poetry collections with *en face* translations into Irish, many of them undertaken by Liam Prút. The most recent Coiscéim volumes are Crìsdean MacIlleBhàin's (Christopher Whyte) *Dealbh Athar* (2009) and Màiri NicGumaraid's *Fo Stiùir a Faire* (2012). Irish poet Gréagóir Ó Dúill, who produced the Irish versions of MacIlleBhàin's poems, has given a detailed insight into the interactive, back-and-forth, give-and-take creative process involved in their production, describing his role as "facilitator rather than translator", given the linguistic proximity of Irish and Scottish Gaelic.

These bilingual Gaelic-Irish editions are comparable to Gaelic-English editions in the sense that they provide the only platform in which the Gaelic poems are presented to the Gaelic readership in Scotland, but the Irish text is less culturally overpowering and more linguistically enriching. In contrast, translations of already-published Gaelic poems into other European languages are intended for foreign readerships and have a different function. Iain Galbraith's major volume of modern Scottish poetry into German, *Beredter Norden: Schottische Lyrik seit 1900* (2011), includes more than 20 Gaelic poems, most of them translated by Corinna Krause. Catriona Zoltowska and Antonio Rivero Taravillo's *Canciones gaélicas* (2002) is a bilingual Gaelic-Spanish edition of 26 songs and poems from the sixteenth to the eighteenth century, drawing mostly on the women's song tradition. An intermediate category is translation of Gaelic poetry into Scots, an important phenomenon of recent years, as with Derrick McClure's translations of Somhairle MacGill-Eain's *Dàin do Eimhir* (*Sangs tae Eimhir* (2011)) and Aonghas Pàdraig Caimbeul's *Meas air chrannaibh/Fruit on brainches/Fruit on branches*, published trilingually in 2007.

10

Contemporary poet Rody Gorman (who also produces original poetry in Irish) has challenged the concept of translation itself in his recent collection *Beartan Briste agus dàin Ghàidhlig eile* (2011), which bears the remarkable English title *Burstbroken Judgementshroudloomdeeds and other Gaelic poems*. Gorman's central device is simple but is pushed to its limits and beyond: he plays on the notoriously polysemous definitions of Edward Dwelly's celebrated *Gaelic-English Dictionary*, published in 1911, by squeezing multiple different possible translations of individual Gaelic words into his English versions. Thus Dwelly's entry for *beart*, as used in the title of the collection and its first Gaelic poem, gives 'judgement', 'shroud', 'loom' or 'deed'; indeed, had Gorman pushed things even further, he could have added no fewer than ten additional meanings for *beart* from Dwelly, including 'harness', 'scabbard', and 'threatening'. The effect varies: sometimes the additional Gaelic meanings Gorman extracts are not obvious, indeed may be thoroughly obscure, to most Gaelic speakers, and so give an unexpected richness of possibilities that the Gaelic reader would not otherwise have considered, while in other cases the overloading of incompatible alternatives renders the English text almost incomprehensible, at least to those without Gaelic, as in the poem "Gathan" (translated as 'sheafspokesunbeamdarts'):

A' siubhal air ais dhomh
Sa Chuan Sgìth,
Chunnaic mi mar lasair
Eadar dà-thaigh solais
Losgadh air an uachdar
Agus de ghathan a' boillsgeadh
Nam faileas
Ann am blobhsag a' bhodaich.

deathseektravellingback in the tiredminchoceanbay,
i saw like a flashflame eitherbothbetween two
moonphaseknowledgelighthouses shootburning on the
woofcreamsurfacetop and sheafspokesunbeamdarts
gaudyglittering like a shadow in the
halfbottlespectreoldcodboy's oilskinblouse.

11

Here the Gaelic text initially seems fairly unambiguous and the Gaelic reader would not normally contemplate any meaning other than 'travelling' for *siubhal* in the first line or 'Minch' for *Cuan Sgìth* in the second. Rather than using translation to produce a version of an intelligible text that is intelligible in another language, Gorman's "translations" arguably serve to render an intelligible text less intelligible while also producing a second text that is intelligible (if at all) only to those who can read the language of the original text.

Although in demographic terms Gaelic continues to decline, the range of Gaelic use is more diverse than ever before, and the role of the written word (typically written on an electronic screen of some kind) is becoming ever more important. As bilingualism, language-mixing, code-switching and interlinguality become the norm, especially for younger Gaelic speakers whose connection to the language may have little to do with family origin, processes of translation and interaction between languages may play an increasingly important role. Translation will probably become a more complex and variegated affair, not just a straightforward process of transfer from one language to another. At the same time, existential questions are omnipresent: will Gaelic survive? how will it be used? why should it be used? why should it survive? These questions give a great deal of scope for creative responses.

Further Reading

McLeod, Wilson. "The Packaging of Gaelic Poetry". *Chapman* 89-90 (1998): 149-51.

—. "Official Gaelic: Problems in the Translation of Public Documents". *Scottish Language*, 19 (2000): 100-16.

Dymock, Emma and Wilson McLeod, eds. *Lainnir a' Bhùirn/The Shining Water: Essays on Modern Gaelic Literature*. Edinburgh: Dunedin Academic Press, 2011.

Whyte, Christopher. "Translation as Predicament". *Translation and Literature* 9 (2000): 179-87.

—. "Against Self-Translation". *Translation and Literature* 11 (2002): 64-71.

"Maister Francis Villon" and the Translations of Tom Scott, William J. Tait, and Norman Cameron

Richie McCaffery

The poetry of François Villon, the fifteenth-century French poet, thief, killer, *mauvais garçon* and *poète maudit*, was translated by a number of twentieth-century Scottish poets, in particular poets who were writing in the post-war second wave of the Scottish Literary Renaissance. This renaissance is most commonly associated with Hugh MacDiarmid (1892 – 1978), who is thought of as its progenitor in the immediate aftermath of World War One. At first a movement of linguistic and poetic rejuvenation in the writing of Scots, this almost militaristic literary campaign developed over the years to include the translation of poetry from many languages into Scots in a bid to construct a renewed national identity, fuelled in part by broadening its horizons with a more international perspective. Scottish poets Tom Scott (1918 – 1995), William J. Tait (1919 – 1992) and Norman Cameron (1905 – 1953) all produced translations of Villon in some of the more predominant dialects and languages of Scotland. I will compare a selection of these and identify some of the reasons why Villon was in particular considered such a pertinent voice for translation.

Tom Scott had an early flirtation with the short-lived New Apocalypse movement, the 1930s and 1940s' surrealist and expressionist reaction against the socio-political poetry of Auden, Spender and MacNeice. Much of this early work, written in a

13

densely bardic fashion, was disowned by Scott who said he found his voice in Scots through early translations of Villon. John Herdman writes that Scott's translations of Villon formed "part of his apprenticeship in the composition of Scots poetry, but are of considerable value in their own right". It may strike the reader as odd that Scott's move into Scots translation was not actuated by Hugh MacDiarmid, but by another great modernist mandarin, T. S. Eliot. Scott, in an interview with Joy Hendry in 1992, remembers the inception of his interest in Villon and Eliot's encouragement:

> Pound said they were the best Villon in either Scots or English. Eliot directed me to them... that wee quatrain. Eliot pounced on it and said 'That is the best translation of that I've seen', and encouraged me to do more Villon.

Endorsements, such as that of Eliot above, show that while these translations may be comical or bawdy in their original and translated forms, it is the intentions of the translator which are serious and committed to demonstrating poetic excellence. These are not merely poets "trying their hand" at translation, but using both the form and content of Villon's work as a means to either cement or explore a literary Scots identity through the use of Scots, Shetlandic or standard English as a legitimate poetic medium. The historical distance between Villon and these poets is not enough of a reason to explain their collective appropriation of his oeuvre, there must be something within the work which, intellectually and emotionally, speaks to these poets as relevant and worthy of recovery.

William J. Tait is recognized for his work in an Edinburgh-Shetlandic crossover dialect. Tait's output was very small, but a significant portion of this was made up of translations of Villon into a Shetlandic dialect. Although both Scott and Tait were well known to each other, Norman Cameron was not acquainted with either of these poets and yet his interest in translating Villon was just as profound, while his methods and style differed. Cameron is still unfairly regarded as the satellite and foil of Dylan Thomas and an acolyte of Robert Graves. Jonathan Baker writes of Cameron: "by remaining just outside the mainstream [...] Cameron's work appears

today less damaged by changes in literary styles." Cameron was a
Scottish poet but spent most of his short life as a rootless expatriate.
His versions are tight, spare and elegant and offer a vivid contrast to
Scott's Lallans and Tait's Shetlandic. It is only by looking closely at
these different versions that we can begin to appreciate the qualities
in Villon's work that appealed so much to the modern outlook of
these poets.

Tom Scott uses one of Villon's shorter poems, a mere quatrain
(the one so admired by Eliot) as an epigraph to his collection. Both
jokey and deadly serious, literally an example of "gallows" or gallus
humour, it lends itself well to a rendering in Scots and is worth
quoting in full:

> I am France's, born o stock
> Native tae Paris, Pontoise folk.
> Sae, tae tie up this French joke,
> Ma neck maun learn the weicht o ma dock.

The masculine rhymes in Scots give it a blunt, witty feel, but it is
worth remembering that Villon was sentenced to death by hanging,
only to have his punishment reduced to banishment from Paris at
the last moment. Norman Cameron's version of this same poem is
entitled "Je Suis François…" and, although longer, it manages to
pull off more elaborate homophonous word-play while still retaining
a sense of the vulgar and demotic:

> Francis by name, France's by birth
> (I never had much luck on earth),
> At Paris first I op'd my eyes
> (It is a hamlet near Pontoise);
> And soon my neck, to end this farce,
> Must learn how heavy is my arse.

While Cameron seems to get the balance right between the
acrolect and the colloquial here, his version of "Lay" or "Rondel",
a poignant short elegy for a dead lover, loses some of the pathos to

Tait's version. Cameron translates in a curiously stiff and overblown way:

> Death, of thy rigour I complain:
> Hast ravished my mistress hence,
> And wilt not yet show penitence,
> But holdest me in swooning pain,
> With all my vital forces ta'en.
> How did her life give thee offence,
>   Death?

While Cameron conveys the impression all too melodramatically of a man driven mad by grief, it is Tait's version which carries a heart-rending plea to "Daeth":

> Daeth, I curse dy cruel hand
> At took da lass I loved fae me
> An yit will no contentit be,
> Less I stey longsome i da land
> O weary livin an demaand
> What faat shu ever did ta dee,
>   Daeth.

Cameron's version begs for an answer, Tait's is more of a wounded soliloquy which accepts that the poem is rhetorical, and will not be answered by "Daeth". It reminds the reader of the voice of Orpheus in Goodsir Smith's *Under the Eildon Tree*, who, having loved, lost and found to lose again "Euridicie", laments that "Aa this will happen aa again / Monie and monie a time again".

'The Ballade of Fat Margie' is easily Villon's most scabrous poem, where the poet shares a highly volatile and drink-fuelled relationship with a fat Parisian demirep. The poem is about the civilized face they try to put on when entertaining guests and the lubricious reality of their private lives. After a blazing row, they make up and in Cameron's version the language wavers between genteelism, euphemism and ribald satiation:

> Then peace is made and she lets flee a fart,
> Like an envenom'd beetle all a-bloat,
> And lays her hand upon my privy part.

Tait's version of "Fat Margret's Ballade" is certainly an amusing and racy incarnation, but it focuses too much on the gross humour of the scene, using much more scatological language to make this apparent:

> Laachin, she lays her hand on me, an: "Start!
> Vite! Vite!" she says, an gies my prick a nug…
>
> As we laek shaarn, shite shaests wis shoen an late.
> We skail fae honor, an hit's joest as blate…

It is Tom Scott's "A Ballat O Fat Margie" which strikes a winning mix of archaism and blunt masculine rhymes that move between high and low linguistic registers, between the "huirshop" and "consort an queen":

> Lauchs, sits doun on ma waim an feels ma pairt;
> Says "go on", giein ma middle-leg a puhll.
> Fair drunk, we sleep lik logs whaur I first fell.
> At dawn, her raandy quim complainin syne,
> She clims on me afore her sun can dwyne;
> Eftir a rub or twa I groan wi pain;
> Her weicht fair spiles whit little pleasure's mine,
> In this huirshop whaur, consort an queen, we reign.

While all three poets are involved in a process of reclaiming and reworking Villon to bring him closer to their chosen languages and dialects, it is Scott who invests and immerses himself wholly in the translation of Villon. He explains his *modus operandi* as not merely a way "to work in my own style, my language" or to use "somebody else as a ladder to climb to where I should have been" but to re-establish a vital link with the Scottish literary canon.

We can clearly see this process of appropriation of Villon in Scott's translation of one of Villon's most famous poems, "Ballat o the Leddies o Langsyne". Stephen P. Smith writes that Tom Scott subjects Villon to "the alchemy of Scots" and praises his "ability to appropriate the foreign for his own purposes". In Cameron's English version of the same poem ("Ballade of the Ladies of Bygone Time"), he preserves the phrase most commonly associated with Villon within the English language, the refrain "Where are the snows of yesteryear?" In contrast, in Scott's rendering we are exposed to echoes of the rhetoric of the medieval makars and of the eighteenth-century Scots of Robert Burns and Robert Fergusson:

> Tell me whaur, in whit countrie
> Bides Flora nou, yon Roman belle?
> Whaur Thais, Alcibiades be,
> Thon sibbit cuisins: can ye tell
> Whaur cletteran Echo draws pell-mell
> Abuin some burn owrehung wi bine
> Her beautie's mair nor human spell –
> Ay, whaur are the snaws o langsyne?

If we contrast this version in Scots, which has a clear linguistic and nationalist agenda, with the English rendering of a "rootless" expatriate Scottish poet, we see a poem that is strangely stilted, one that tries to give a sense of the cadences of a voice from the past but with little intention beyond a display of poetic craftsmanship:

> Tell me where, beneath what skies
> Is lovely Roman Flora ta'en?
> Tell me where Archipiada lies,
> Or Thais (they were kin, these twain);
> Or Echo, answering again
> Across the river and the mere,
> Beauty of more than human strain?
> Where are the snows of yesteryear?

Often Cameron's versions are more tentative than Scott's assertive translations, yet they ask more questions of the reader. Although Cameron's are perhaps more faithful and understated, Scott's are firm, purposeful and rigid. Scott's version of the envoi to this poem is masterly in its seamless absorption of Villon's message into a Scots tongue which is as aware of the poets of the past as it is of its individualism. In Scott's hands the poem is evocative of the snows and voices of yesteryear, and it is perhaps this quality of belatedness that appealed to Eliot:

> Prince, this week I cannae well,
> Nor this year, say whaur nou they shine:
> Speir, ye'll but hear the owrecome swell
> Ay, whaur are the snaws o langsyne?

This is not to belittle Cameron's achievement, as in the quiet dexterity of his English versions we can arguably see him enacting his own experience and intentions, albeit in a much less palpable way than Scott. Cameron's versions clearly seem to hail from the past, but within this they are rather detached. In many ways, while Scott is trying to clearly orientate and pin down his take on Villon within the Scottish Literary Renaissance, it is in fact Cameron's floating status within established schools or movements of twentieth century poetry which is more in keeping with Villon's itinerant and outcast image, and this quality is attained in Cameron's rather disconnected translations into English.

Similarly, and poignantly, in Tait's original poetry we recurrently encounter a man drinking alone in a pub, occasionally catching glimpses of himself in a mirror as "an overweight deracinated Shetlander" ("Racial Characteristics: A Cautionary Tale"). Tait, for all his boozy and rollicking versions of Villon, is as physically dispossessed as Cameron and Villon, and he uses English, Scots and Shetlandic to denote degrees of alienation, separation or, as Douglas Dunn has written, "literary loneliness". In this light, Tait's Shetlandic renderings of Villon become redemptive acts of what Dunn has called "poetic ingenuity and linguistic adventure".

Villon's poetry projects images of the poet as a man on the run and a man facing up to his prosecutors and punishment as a means of speaking about his own mortality. All three Scots poets have versions of Villon's *Ballade* written from the perspective of the dead at the gallows, where six executed men plead for clemency from God, not just for themselves, but for mankind. Cameron's version in heightened English has the air of a courtroom appeal for mercy to "guard us from Satan's wicked signory". It is in fact the colloquial spoken-word immediacy and imagery of Tait's and Scott's versions which strike the reader as appeals from poor wretches at the gallows. Tait's style lends itself well to the passionate and vocal plea to the common spectator:

> O bridder men, livin as eence did we,
> Hae nae hard herts at wis, fur as ye tak
> Peety on wir black sowls da Loard'll be
> Gligger ta blenk an ee sood yours be black.
> Here see wir crangs hing, five or sax;
> As fur da flesh we oesed ta feed owre weel,
> Maidin wi wirms, it's scaffed noo, every peel;
> Ta moeld an ess wir dry banes waste awa.
> Lit nae man mock dem as dey dirl an sweel,
> Bit pray da Loard at He'll furgie wis aa.

While Tait's rendering into a Shetlandic parlance adds a striking vocalic dimension to the poem, it is Scott's version of the poem which is direct, impassioned and strongly visual:

> We hae been washed and purifee'd by rain.
> The sun hes tanned our hides a leathery hue.
> Craws and pyes hae pykit out our een,
> And barbered ilka stibble-chin and brou...
>
> Mair stoggit nor straeberries, and juist as raw.
> See til it ye never mell wi sic a crew,
> And pray the Lord shaws mercy til us aa.

Tait's and Scott's renderings of the more serious Villon poems into Shetlandic and Scots seem to capture more of what Scott calls the "great pathos and tenderness in Villon" than the august but rather sterile English versions of Cameron. In the same interview with Tom Scott, Joy Hendry claims that "The Scots language always strikes me as being so inherently dramatic, partly because of the rhythm and sound of it." In the case of Scott's version of "Ballat o the Hingit", the profoundly dramatic subject matter is that of eternal shriving or damnation of the condemned, and the appeal of the "hingit" to the crowd belongs in an impassioned and colloquial register, not the rarefied English of Cameron.

This comparison of a selection of translated poems these poets have in common shows that the gravitas of Cameron's English works better when applied to the more subversive and "miry" aspects of Villon. His language could be considered an "authentic" English approximation of the original, and Villon's bawdy and bohemian spirit is amply captured in "Je Suis François". Both Tait and Cameron share Villon's existential status as that of the drifting or runaway poet. Whereas Cameron's versions give little clue as to his past or location – they are in fact forms of escape from the ego of the translator – Tait's Shetlandic renderings show both origin and displacement.

However, it is Scott who most ambitiously manipulated Villon's poetry in order to serve his own apprenticeship in the literary potential of Scots and there have been correspondingly high opinions of his achievements. Duncan Glen, for instance, has hailed Scott's Villon as "one of the high peaks of 20th Century poetry". Scott himself argues that "the *gradus ad Parnassum* is translate, imitate, emulate, create" and that his poems are "dominated by a family heredity". Scott always denied that his versions of Villon were "translations" at all, but individual recreations, new poems in themselves that "belong to the translator".

While Scott's Scots and Tait's Shetlandic are better equipped to tackle Villon's sweeping use of both prestige and colloquial registers, it is the seriousness of Scott's effort that seems to lose some of the populism and humour of Villon's message. Cameron by contrast seems to capture Villon's wit and wordplay with ease, but his desire to interact with and connect to Villon's growing Catholic faith comes across as occasionally stiff and stilted.

Each poet's aim in translating or "recreating" Villon may appear to be different, but intrinsically all three present Villon as a poet relevant to the twentieth century. In doing so, they bring both outsider reputations and languages into the centre of literary discussion and readership within a Scottish literary scene which in itself occupies, and either flourishes or withers on, the periphery of "English literature". It seems to have been a serious and salutary exercise for all three of these poets to see a life of such hardship lived out against such societal resistance as that of Villon, whose work speaks vigorously and lustily for his time. The poverty and yet poetic richness of Villon's life and work speaks to Norman Cameron particularly as one of wandering and rootlessness.

However, it is the translations of Scott and Tait which try for the first time to tether Villon to a certain canon and movement. The dark second life of Villon also speaks to the split of language and identity of the writer in modern Scotland, and of the cultural depredations Scotland has seen in the centuries following Villon's death. The appeal and resonance of Villon's oeuvre go beyond the similarities of "gallows humour", second life, use of prestige and demotic language, poverty, precariousness and the "Auld Alliance". These poets did not merely translate as a demonstration of crafts-manship, they translated to invest emotionally in the existential bent of Villon's work and in doing so, each found a voice of his own. Cameron, Scott and Tait are presently obscure and marginalized poets, as Villon once was, but one hopes that in turn their work will be re-discovered as part of a vital tradition in Scotland that has survived because it thrives on the periphery.

A Cresseid for Our Time: Seamus Heaney's Translation of Henryson

Morna Fleming

W hen the great Scottish poet Robert Henryson wrote his *Testament of Cresseid* in the late fifteenth century, he relieved Geoffrey Chaucer's heroine from the obscurity in which she had been left in the English poet's *Troilus and Criseyde*. Henryson gave her a continuing life as a very Scottish Cresseid, condemned by the gods to end her days as a leper in punishment for her "insolence, … play and wantones" (l. 319. Line numbers are taken from Denton Fox's (Oxford, 1987) edition of the poems). Now, more than half a millennium after Henryson, one of our greatest contemporary poets, Seamus Heaney, has taken a fresh look at the woman who has become a byword for faithlessness and sexual lust, and has, in his translation of *The Testament* given us a Cresseid for our time.

The story of Troilus and Criseyde/Cressida is probably best known from either Chaucer's fourteenth-century narrative poem or Shakespeare's seventeenth-century drama. Briefly, the story concerns the love between Troilus, a warrior of Troy and Cressida, the daughter of the Trojan seer/priest Calchas who defected to the Greeks. After consummating their love, Cressida is summoned back to the Greek camp in exchange for a Trojan prisoner, Antenor. Cressida vows that she will remain faithful to Troilus, but she accepts the Greek warrior Diomedes' love and abandons all thought of returning to Troy. Shakespeare heightens the drama and the tragedy by having Troilus witness Cressida's betrayal in the act, while Chaucer simply draws a veil over the outcome, leaving Troilus to realize eventually that he will not see his lover again.

While Henryson imagines "ane uther quair" in addition to Chaucer's poem in which he found the continuing story of Cresseid, Heaney relates directly to his source text, printing the Middle Scots version on facing pages to his translation to enable readers to make a comparison, and to make a bridge between the two versions. However, he uses the word "retelling" when translating Henryson's "tragedie", indicating that this will not be an exact translation, but a version of the source text. Readers will find that this retelling is significantly influenced by Heaney's own experiences in the divided community of Northern Ireland and by contemporary moral attitudes to female sexuality.

Heaney was attracted to the work both for the pleasure of the translation itself and for his desire to bring Henryson "out of the university syllabus and on to the shelves". As he says in the introduction to his translation, he enjoyed working on the poem as it took him back into what he calls "the hidden Scotland at the back of [his] own ear ... the Ulster Scots idioms and pronunciations" familiar from his youth that inspired him to begin putting "the not very difficult Scots language of his 'originals' into rhymed stanzas of more immediately accessible English". There has always been a strongly Scots voice in Ulster, and since devolution matters Scottish have come to the foreground. Canongate's *An Leabhar Mòr* (2002), an anthology of verse and artwork from Ireland and Scotland which includes Heaney's "Pangur Bàn", exemplifies this interest and cross-fertilization.

As in Heaney's award-winning translation of the Anglo-Saxon *Beowulf* (1999), the archaic forms and structures are melded with a contemporary idiom which brings the work into today's world while preserving the essential strangeness of the setting and characters. "Henryson is a narrative poet whom you read not only for the story but for the melody of understanding in the storytelling voice ... [where] the phonetic make-up contributes strongly if stealthily to the emotional power of the declaration," Heaney explains. He admits that, right from the opening stanza, "[his] own sense-clearing could not hope to capture fully that tolling tragic note" but could only "echo the metre and approximate the rhyme", while intending to "match as far as possible the rhetoric and roguery of the originals, and in general 'keep the accent'". While employing the rime royal structure introduced by Chaucer and continued by Henryson, Heaney frequently adopts formal elements of traditional Irish poetry, including assonant rhyme and alliteration.

The poem's opening in a blasted spring, when a sudden cold spell has driven the narrator to the warmth of the fire is, in Middle Scots: "The *froist freisit*, the *blastis bitterly*/Fra Pole Artick come *quhisling loud and schill*" (ll. 19-20, emphasis mine). Heaney here shows exactly what he means by "the not very difficult Scots language of the original" in a translation which requires very little adaptation to read naturally: "The *frost froze* hard, the *blast* came *bitterly*/From the pole-star, *whistling loud and shrill*", where the alliteration and onomatopoeia echo the sounds of the source text as well as the northerly wind. Cresseid and the poet-narrator are spiritual siblings, the former suffering the effects of the coldness of abandonment, and the latter the coldness of old age, and the poet-narrator hopes that the story of Cresseid may in some way rejuvenate him: "For I traistit that Venus, luifis queen,/*My faidit hart of lufe* scho *wald make grene*" (ll. 23-4). Heaney translates this as "I had placed my trust in Venus, as love's queen/.../That she should *sprig my fallow heart with green*", a natural image suggesting the new growth of spring, the long time passed since the experience of love, and the colour of youth and Venus herself.

Becoming absorbed in his reading, the poet-narrator finds Cresseid, following her abandonment by Diomedes, lamenting her lot: "Now am I *maid* ane unworthy *outwaill*,/And all in *cair* transl*ait* is my joy" (ll. 129-30) which becomes "I have been *demeaned* into an *outcast*,/Transl*at*ed and betr*ay*ed out of my joy." This Cresseid blames in the previous line on the gods "who once divinely promised/That I would be the flower of love in Troy" (ll. 127-8). The slant rhyme of "promised" and "outcast" emphasizes the latter word, while the assonance in "Transl*at*ed" and "betr*ay*ed" reinforces Cresseid's despair at her situation.

As Cresseid begins her complaint against Venus and Cupid, Henryson says "doun in ane *exstasie/ravischit in spreit*, intill ane dreame scho fell," (ll. 141-2) which Heaney renders as "her *spirits ebbed away/In a fainting fit* and into dream she fell". The word "ravischit" has, for the medieval writer, connotations of an overwhelming spiritual experience conveying an oracular message and is virtually untranslatable. Heaney neatly circumvents this by imagining Cresseid stripped of her own consciousness and overpowered by the dream, within which he produces a tour de force of poetic description of the catalogue of the gods. The figure of Mars is particularly fine, and in some ways surpasses the "original", as in the line "*Wrything* his face with *mony angrie word*," (l. 189) which is rendered with many more verbs and heightened by the internal rhyme: "And raged, grimaced, rampaged and bawled and scoffed." The description of Venus with her "insinuating becks and glances" (l. 226), using the Scots and Ulster Scots word "beck" for an inviting look, reminds us of the narrator's wistful hope at the opening of the poem as she rules over love which is: "Now grene as leif, now widderit and ago" l. 238), translated as "Now green in leaf, now withered on the bough."

The gods' sentence on Cresseid, to curse her with leprosy, would, in Henryson's day, have been seen as appropriate, as it was thought to be a venereal disease caused by worshipping Venus in sexual love. Henryson gives a very clear depiction of a leprous face, which Cresseid, reviving from her swoon: "... saw ... sa *deformait,/Gif scho in hart was wa* aneuch, God wait!" (ll. 344-5). Heaney shows a matching sympathy for the devastated woman: "And when she saw her face ... so *ruined/God* knows if she was not *heartsore* and stunned," adding to her horror and ending the line once again on an assonant rhyme which heightens the dramatic effect.

Cresseid's formal complaint, which Heaney translates as "lament", spoken on her first night in the leper house, is a beautifully rendered set piece which uses the modern idiom skilfully while incorporating the alliteration and the *aabaabbab* rhyme scheme, a new feature in this section of the source text:

'O sop of sorrow, sonkin into cair! ...
Of all blythness now art thou blaiknit bair;

Thair is na salve may saif or sound thy sair!
Fell is thy fortoun, wickit is thy weird,
Thy blys is baneist, and thy baill on breird!
Under the earth, God gif I gravin wer,
Qhuair nane of Grece nor yit of Troy micht heird!'
(ll. 406-15)

Heaney renders this virtually word for word, but with significant alterations to clarify the sense:

'O sop of sorrow, sunk and steeped in care! ...
There is no salve can heal or soothe your sore.
Your spirit flags that was flushed up before.
Your fate will doom you, destiny destroy.
Your bliss is banished and fresh fears annoy.
God send me under earth, down through death's door
Where no-one's heard the name of Greece or Troy.'

He retains the archaic essence of the source text by melding heavy alliteration with contemporary collocations to create a fluent and natural translation. Similarly, the final two lines of the formal complaint, "Be war thairfoir, approchis neir the hour:/Fortoun is fickle quhen scho beginnis and steiris!" (ll. 468-9), are rendered as "Beware therefore in time. The hour draws close/And fate is fickle when she plies the shears." In the final line, the conflation of Henryson's Fortune with Heaney's allusion to the god of Fate Atropos, who wields the shears of life and death, is a particularly beautiful image.

Cresseid's second lament gives us her remembrance of Troylus: "For lufe of me thow *keipt gude continence,*/Honest and chaist in *conversation*" (ll. 554-5), which Heaney renders as "For love of me you *kept desire reined in,*/Honourable and chaste in your *behaviour.*" This is an instance where the shifts from the source text are absolutely essential to convey the sense to a modern reader, to whom terms like "continence" and "conversation" have quite different meanings from those ascribed by Henryson. A similar rationale can be observed in Heaney's rendering of "[Of all women protectour and

27

defence]/Thou was, and *keipit thair opinioun*," (ll. 546-7) as "their good names' guarantor".

The foregoing remarks have highlighted some significant features of diction in Heaney's translation, and the use of a type of rhyme which is common in Irish poetry, but there are subtler aspects to be discerned. Allusions to sectarian difference can be found in many of Heaney's poems, and his collections *Wintering Out* (1973) and *North* (1975) seek to interweave commentary on "The Troubles" with a historical context and wider human experience. The same kind of allusion is seen for the first time in the translation when Cresseid returns to her father's house, where Heaney has her going "beyond the line/To a splendid mansion in the Greek-held quarter" (ll. 95-6), carrying the sense of the lines of demarcation between two armies, or between two communities, where Heaney puts Cresseid into a position of involuntary vulnerability. This additional dimension is not present in Henryson, where she simply "passit far out of the toun/Ane myle or twa, unto ane mansioun." To press the point further, when Cresseid is condemned by the gods, Heaney again makes a significant change to the source text. The entire sense of Henryson's lines: "… in all hir lyfe with pane to be opprest,/And torment sair with seikness incurabill,/And to all lovers be abhominabill," (ll. 306-8) is there in "She would live in painful torment from then on/By lovers be despised, abominable,/*Beyond the pale*, diseased, incurable." The Pale, as the English-colonized area around Dublin was originally known, gives us the expression "beyond the Pale" for something totally unacceptable, barbaric and foreign. For Heaney as an Ulsterman, this is a particularly powerful expression. This is where he locates Grendel in his translation of *Beowulf*, and also the narrator figure in *Stations*. In doing so he conveys a very specific kind of exclusion to exemplify Cresseid's loss of community through the sentence of leprosy passed on her.

The final stanzas of the translation once again show how Heaney recontextualizes the tale in an Irish setting. Henryson's "Quhen he had hard hir greit infirmitie,/Hir legacie and *lamentatioun*," (ll.596-7) is given as "When he had listened to the whole story/Of her ordeal, her *keen*, her testament," where the use of the word "keen", redolent of Irish lament, takes the reader into the death-room. These are subtle points, but they show how the classical setting of the source text is reframed to reflect a divided Ulster and empathize with Cresseid's abjectness.

The empathy shown by Heaney for his heroine is also in contrast to Henryson's rather conventional medieval attitude, which tends to divide women into Mary or Eve, virgin or whore. While Henryson's aged narrator does at times show an uncharacteristic sympathy for Cresseid in her abandonment, Heaney develops this into an even more empathic and realistically psychological response, in which Cresseid is seen as the victim rather than the agent of her downfall.

In the translation of Henryson's "Quhen Diomede had *all his appetite,/And mair*, fulfillit of this fair ladie," (ll. 71-2) as "When Diomede had *sated his desire/And oversated* it on this fair lady," the repetition of "sated" and "oversated" echoes the sense of Diomedes' lustful gluttony; further, the alliteration stresses the finality of Cresseid's banishment from her former protector: "And sent Cresseid a *ban*ishment decree/To *bind* and *bar* her from his company" (ll. 74-5). Heaney's rendering of Henryson's "desolait" (l. 76) as "distracted and would ramble" rather than the straightforward "desolate" suggests a more pathetic mental wandering as well as aimless walking. In the final line of this stanza, there is a subtle shift in meaning, when "And *sum men sayis*, into the court, *commoun*" (l. 77) becomes "And be, *as men will say, available*", generalizing the male attitude and beginning to show the woman as helpless prey. Heaney is very alert to the invidious position that Cresseid finds herself in.

Similarly, in the next two stanzas Heaney renders "To change in *filth* all thy *feminitie,/And* be with *fleschlie lust* sa *maculait*" (ll. 80-1) as "*dragged down* as a *woman/And sullied* so by *lustful appetite*", which is very different stylistically, as it preserves the alliteration but changes the active to the passive voice, and suggests an external agent. This echoes Henryson's accusation while at the same time rendering Cresseid the victim rather than the whore. While "like any common pick-up" conveys the tenor of "Sa gigotlike takand thy foull pleasance!" (l. 83), in the source text Cresseid is the instigator of the sexual activity, whereas in the translation, again, she is the passive instrument of men's sexual pleasure. In the last line of that stanza Heaney makes a fairly significant grammatical change, from

Henryson's "*I have pitie* thow suld *fall* sic *mischance*", (l. 84) conveying the idea of Fortune actively intervening in Cresseid's life, to "When I recollect your *fall, I want to weep*." Henryson's "fall" is a verb, which Heaney transforms into a noun, and the development of "I have pitie" into "I want to weep" makes the empathy even more overt.

The following stanza continues the theme, conveying "quhat ever men deme or say/*In scornefull langage* of thy *brukkilnes*" (l. 85-6), using the conventional accusation of "brukkilnes" ('frailty'), as "whatever men may think or say/*Contemptuously* about your *quick compliance*." In this case the final line, jarring in its hard consonants, creates a sense of contrast between the reality of the helpless woman's situation and the stories which are spread by others. Henryson's "The quhilk *fortoun* hes put to sic distress/*As hir pleisit*, and nothing throw the gilt/Of the, *throw wickit langage to be spilt*" (ll. 89-91) becomes "Which the *whim of fortune* put to such distress –/No guilt for it to be attributed/To you, *bad-mouthed by noxious gossip*." In this instance, Heaney has eschewed end rhyme in the couplet in favour of contemporary idiom.

In Cresseid's second lament, when she finally accepts her own part in her fate, Heaney lessens the load of guilt by translating Cresseid's "wantones" (l. 549) as "giddy and loose in loving", which sounds considerably less damning of her, although it has to be acknowledged that in the next stanza there is a much more robust self-accusation. After her description of the faithful Troylus, Heaney's use of alliteration in the fifth line: "But I, with my *hot flesh*, my mind a *fetor,*/Was *lustful, passionate and lecherous*," echoes the source text's "My mynd in *fleschelie foull affectioun*/Was inclynit to *lustis lecherous*" (ll. 558-9) while adding a particularly unattractive aspect to Cresseid's admission.

This brief account of some of the salient features of the translation highlights the skilfulness and effectiveness of Heaney's diction. It is clear that Heaney uses Robert Henryson's poem both as an authority and a springboard for creation, as Henryson used Chaucer's poem. The fluency of the English version, which reads as a new poem in its own right, effectively revives the medieval poem for a new cultural audience. Heaney encourages readers to address Henryson in the "original", as the Middle Scots text has been regularized in terms of orthography to make it as easy to read as possible. Heaney's very subtle references to the divided Ulster recontextualizes the classical setting of the source text, and reframes Cresseid's abjectness in contemporary terms. In his moderation of Henryson's medieval attitudes, he reveals an empathy which recasts Cresseid without moral judgement. Heaney shows that Henryson still has a claim to relevance for Scots, English and Irish readers, that his work has a universality that transcends the centuries since its creation, and that his characters and situations can be appreciated in our own time.

Further Reading

Henryson, Robert. *The Testament of Cresseid & Seven Fables*. Trans. Seamus Heaney. London: Faber & Faber, 2009.

Enlightened Reception?
Scottish Texts in Asian Languages

Dennis Smith

In 2001 Arthur Herman raised some eyebrows with his book *How the Scots Invented the Modern World: the True Story of How Western Europe's Poorest Nation Created Our World & Everything in It* (a title subsequently toned down for the UK market). Perhaps a modest pinch of salt is in order: modernity takes many forms, not all of which have obviously Scottish roots. But it is certainly true that the literati of the Scottish Enlightenment told a striking tale. They were hardly unanimous in their views (the Scots are notoriously disputatious) but many subscribed to a theory of co njectural or stadial history which claimed that human life is governed by natural laws which lead all societies, at differing paces, through the same developmental stages, culminating in commercial modernity.

These ideas have been immensely influential. They underlay the once-dominant Whig interpretation of history and fed, through their influence on Hegel, Marx and others, into a much wider European tradition. This article looks at one small link in this chain of dissemination, the role of translations of non-fictional Scottish writing before 1900 in disseminating ideas of modernity in various Asian cultures.

The research data used are drawn from the online Bibliography of Scottish Literature in Translation (BOSLIT) which is available through the National Library of Scotland website at www.nls.uk/catalogues/boslit. BOSLIT records over 30,000 translations into more than 70 different languages. For the twentieth and twenty-first centuries BOSLIT focuses narrowly on literature in the modern sense – mainly fiction, poetry and drama. But for earlier periods (particularly the eighteenth century) it interprets literature in its older sense which enabled David Hume, Adam Smith and their fellow "philosophers" to see themselves as members of a transnational "republic of letters". It was only later, under the influence of Romanticism and scientific specialization, that this cosmopolitan world fractured along linguistic and disciplinary lines. Paralleling these changes, BOSLIT coverage of non-fiction tapers off over the nineteenth century, limiting its scope to non-fiction written by "literary" authors and widely read public intellectuals.

The article is by no means a comprehensive study of all Scottish texts in Asian languages. BOSLIT's own coverage is deliberately limited but also unintentionally skewed by its dependence on external catalogues and bibliographical resources. Broadly speaking, its coverage deteriorates as it moves beyond the core European languages. Some Asian languages, notably Chinese and Japanese, are well recorded in mainstream resources like OCLC WorldCat, but others are not. Without specialist linguistic resources some Indian and south-east Asian languages are hard to access.

In addition, some individuals and topics are consciously avoided. For example, Thomas Carlyle does not fit neatly into any vision of modernity: he was a contrarian who can be read as a prophet of the counter-Enlightenment. In addition, Robert Louis Stevenson's relationship with the South Seas, both in fiction and non-fiction, is too complex to discuss here. Scottish missionary activity (one of Stevenson's concerns) and the whole relationship of religion to modernity are also omitted, as is the role of fiction (notably Scott's novels) in transmitting Enlightenment ideas.

A number of key figures can be discussed here in relation to modernity. A good starting-point is Major-General Sir John Malcolm, hardly a household name but definitely a larger than life personality, whose career was also representative of wider social and intellectual trends. As the fourth son of a minor laird he had to make his own way in the world. The *Oxford Dictionary of National Biography* (ODNB) describes him as "daring and venturesome ('the scapegrace and scapegoat of the family')" – quite an accolade when two of his brothers ended up as knighted admirals. Leaving school at twelve he went straight into the service of the East India Company where he distinguished himself as a soldier, linguist and diplomat. By the age of thirty he was the Company's envoy to the Shah of Persia (who tried to recruit his services).

Malcolm was both a man of action and an author. His *History of Persia*, drawing on personal experience as well as wide learning, appeared in 1815 and was quickly translated into French, Italian and German. By 1867 at the latest it had also appeared in Persian and quickly became a standard historical source, frequently reprinted in India as well as Iran. His *Political History of India* and his *Memoir of Central India* were also translated, into Urdu. Malcolm also had conventional literary ambitions: his volumes of verse include *Persia: a Poem* (1814) which, sadly, does not seem to have been translated.

Malcolm is not an isolated figure: he was part of the Scottish mafia which penetrated the East India Company through the system of patronage perfected by Henry Dundas. And that mafia was itself part of a wider exodus of Scots, relatively well-educated, ambitious and frugal, who went forth to conquer the world, not least the British Empire. Their self-confidence was grounded in an Enlightenment belief in the possibility, if not inevitability, of progress, sometimes reinforced by ideas of divine providence or Calvinist election. These men (and they were overwhelmingly men) were not original thinkers to rank with Hume, Smith and their peers: they were colonial administrators, doctors, merchants, soldiers and explorers. But they had absorbed key principles of Enlightenment thought and they had an immediate influence through their writings as well as their actions.

Similar figures include Mountstuart Elphinstone whose *Account of the Kingdom of Caubul* (1815) was translated into Persian as recently as 1997 and James Fergusson whose *History of Indian and Eastern Architecture* (1867) appeared in Urdu in 1932. John Leyden features in Scottish literature as a poet and folklorist but was also a distinguished linguist and translator, particularly of the *Baburnamah*, the diary of the great sixteenth-century Emperor Babur. This was edited after Leyden's death by his friend William Erskine, whose own *History of India* has also completed its own linguistic loop. Based on a lifetime's study of oriental manuscripts, it was published posthumously and has achieved new life through translations into Persian (1962) and Uzbek (1995).

The key role played by these foot soldiers of the Enlightenment becomes clear when contrasted with the reception of their leaders. David Hume's experience exemplifies the vagaries of reputation. He is now widely recognized as a world-class philosopher, perhaps the greatest to have written in English. Some of his contemporaries agreed: Immanuel Kant, for example, credited Hume with having awoken him from his dogmatic slumbers. But suspicions of atheism and scepticism excluded Hume from the pious halls of the Scottish Common Sense school. As a result, he was best known for many years as a historian and his reputation dipped in the nineteenth century. It was only in the twentieth century that he became a canonical figure in philosophy and his precise place in the Scottish Enlightenment remains controversial. His reception history fits his reputation. BOSLIT does not record any Asian translation before 1900 and his historical writings do not feature at all. As a philosopher he is well represented in Japanese (19 translations), Chinese (16) and Turkish (7). He is notably absent in Korean, otherwise rich in Scottish Enlightenment translations: perhaps suspicions of atheism linger on.

Adam Smith has had a similarly complex afterlife. To his contemporaries, and himself, he was a philosopher, but later generations have redefined him (anachronistically) as an economist and (dubiously) as a prophet of market capitalism. So, it is not surprising that his *Wealth of Nations* reached Asia well before his *Theory of Moral Sentiments*. The first Chinese translation dates from 1902, soon followed by two others. After 1949 the picture is muddied by the diverging paths of mainland China and Taiwan, but a trickle of editions from the 1960s onwards turns into a flood in the twenty-first century, with at least twelve editions and abridgements since 2000. The only recorded Chinese translation of the *Theory of Moral Sentiments* dates from 2004. The *Wealth of Nations* apparently reached Japan later, in 1922, but was assimilated faster, with eight editions before 1950 and a further six in the 1960s alone. Thereafter interest wanes: by then a Smithian interpretation of capitalism had perhaps become commonplace. Again the *Theory of Moral Sentiments* appears later, in 1948, with further editions in 1969 and 1973.

The aforementioned title of Arthur Herman's book implies that all modernity is somehow Scottish. But the chronological variation seen here between the reception of the foot soldiers and the intellectuals suggests that we need to distinguish different aspects of modernity and modernization. In the nineteenth century, with the British Empire at its zenith, Scotland was in reality a beacon of modernity, at the cutting edge in science, technology and medicine as well as industrialization. After the First World War this was no longer true and Scotland went into relative decline. In recent decades, however, the Scottish Enlightenment has come to shine ever more brightly in the academic firmament. Nowadays Scotland is recognized less for its actual modernity than for its historic theorizations of modernity. The translation of Alexander Broadie's *Cambridge Companion to the Scottish Enlightenment* into Chinese in 2010 is a good indication of its current high international profile.

The relationship between modernity and imperialism is complex. It can be used to justify imperialism, in the guise of one society "improving" another and guiding it on the road to enlightened self-determination. (This of course provides no defence of imperialism based on ideas of ineradicable racial difference.) Some translations no doubt fit this imperialist pattern but others were clearly produced by Asians eager to understand Western ideas, whether to adopt them, adapt them or refute them. It may be significant that the vast majority of translations were made by Asians rather than Europeans. In India modernity was initially imposed by invading imperialists on an ethnically, linguistically and culturally diverse subcontinent. In due course, however, Indian intellectuals reacted by developing their own vision of modern secular nationhood.

Things happened differently in Japan, where an already unified state was forced to engage with the outside world by Commodore Perry's ultimatum in 1853. The new imperial government quickly adopted an active policy of modernization through the introduction of Western ideas and technology, with Scotland as one of its main sources. The earliest non-medical translation into Japanese, Alexander Fraser Tytler's *Elements of General History* (published 1801, translated 1871), provides a concise introduction to world history. It was soon followed by popular encyclopaedias like W. & R. Chambers's *Information for the People*. In the 1880s and 1890s Scottish philosophers and political theorists like Alexander Bain, A.J. Balfour and Viscount Bryce start to appear in Japanese. BOSLIT does not cover science, technology and medicine after their development into specialist disciplines, but it seems likely that a similar pattern of reception would be found there as well.

A different aspect of modernization is suggested by the Asian reception of Samuel Smiles, a far from canonical figure in contemporary Scotland. Best known for *Self-help* (published 1859), Smiles was also a prolific biographer, specializing in self-taught Scottish engineers and inventors. BOSLIT records 21 Smiles translations into Chinese, 17 into Japanese and 9 into Korean, almost all recent. He has also been translated into Arabic, Gujarati, Hindi, Persian, Sindhi and Urdu. In terms of rankings he is the second most translated Scottish prose writer in Chinese (after Adam Smith), third in Korean and fifth in Japanese. There is clearly something in Smiles's work that continues to resonate in rapidly industrializing societies. His originally Calvinist values have been seamlessly absorbed into Confucian, Buddhist, Hindu and Muslim cultures, not to mention the quasi-Marxism of contemporary China. Another famously self-made man, Andrew Carnegie, fits the same mould.

A less obvious example is John Stuart Blackie, now remembered chiefly as an eccentric enthusiast for Gaelic, far distant from Smiles's hard-headed utilitarianism. In his own day his international reputation rested mainly on his *On Self Culture, Intellectual, Physical, and Moral* (1874) which was translated into Japanese (1899), Hindi (1904) and Arabic (1906) as well as many European languages. This interest suggests both the prestige of Western education and also a new sense of individual autonomy in traditional societies.

A more quizzical take on modernity, or unchanging human folly, appears in Charles Mackay's *Memoirs of Extraordinary Popular Delusions and the Madness of Crowds*. Mackay had a varied career as a journalist, song-writer and Scottish patriot (and father of the novelist Marie Corelli). The message is spelt out in the title: as well as witch crazes, prophecies and the occult, the book includes case studies of mass economic irrationality like the Dutch tulip mania and the South Sea Bubble. Mackay's book was an immediate best-seller in 1841 and has rarely been out of print since. But apart from an 1871 Dutch translation, BOSLIT records no foreign-language interest before the 1990s when translations sprouted simultaneously in several European and Asian languages. Two separate Chinese translations appeared in 2000, a Turkish abridgement the same year, and a Japanese translation in 2004. We can only speculate how this relates to the dot-com bubble and subsequent market failures.

Translation can also feature as an indirect agent of modernity, that is when one language (e.g. English) acts as an intermediary between others. An intriguing example of this is provided by James Legge, missionary, sinologist, and the first Professor of Chinese at Oxford. The son of an evangelical Huntly draper, he went to China as a Christian missionary but was himself attracted to Confucian values. His magnum opus *Chinese Classics*, published in seven volumes in 1861-72, was crucial in introducing Chinese literature to the Anglophone world. But it played the same role in other cultures as well, not least Japan where Legge's translated texts were widely retranslated into Japanese from 1870 onwards. Metaphorically, Japan came to see China through Scottish spectacles. Another example of an English translation being used as an international conduit of modernity is Henry Yule's compendium of medieval travel writings about China: *Cathay and the Way Thither* (1866). This text was translated into Japanese in 1944 (during the Sino-Japanese war) and reprinted in 1975. No Chinese translation is recorded before 2002.

This role of cultural mediation still carries on. In the light of continuing controversy over the status of Tibet, we might note a 2002 Chinese translation of George Bogle's narrative of his mission in 1774. The first Briton to enter Tibet, Bogle established friendly relations with the Panchen Lama (not to mention at least one Tibetan woman), despite Chinese opposition. In the light of current religious and ethnic tensions in the Xinjiang Uyghur region, we might note a 2006 Chinese translation of Sir William Muir's *The Caliphate: its Rise, Decline and Fall* (published in 1891).

So, this article sees translation as going beyond a simple transposition of a fixed text from one language to another. Texts may be adapted and they (or their adaptations) may migrate through several different languages. Scottish Enlightenment ideas may have reached Asia by a detour through other "imperial" languages, notably French, Dutch and Portuguese in Indo-China and Russian in central Asia. Some Indonesians, for example, probably encountered Scottish authors in Dutch translation. In non-fiction, where ideas and information often come before literary style, the concept of translation becomes indefinitely fluid. Where many speakers are bilingual or multilingual ideas can float free of any particular text or language. This is one reason why Scottish influence in India is essentially unquantifiable, despite the disproportionately large part played by Scots in administering the Raj. Many Scots were fluent in one or more Indian languages while many Indians spoke English.

Ideas, furthermore, can be conveyed through semiotic systems other than language. For instance, the earliest Japanese record in BOSLIT is an 1817 abridgement of William Buchan's international bestseller *Domestic Medicine*. This was apparently mediated through a Dutch text, and thus twice removed from the original. The next record is also medical, a six-volume handbook published in Kyoto around 1822 which references the *Sett of Anatomical Tables* published in 1754 by the man-midwife William Smellie. Again there was a Dutch intermediary, but there may be another difference as well. Smellie's book was famed as much for its plates as for its text, so this may be a case of obstetric information being transmitted through purely graphic means, with no linguistic translation involved at all.

Translation can carry a work far from its original context. As published in 1756 James Ferguson's *Astronomy, Explained on Sir Isaac Newton's Principles* was a mainstream work of Enlightenment natural philosophy. But the Urdu translation published in Ludhiana in 1876 shows Ferguson's method of calculating solar and lunar eclipses being adapted by Hindu astrologers in order to cast horoscopes. Such transformations may conceal a work's original meaning and Scottish roots. This raises an interesting epistemological question: if a Scottish author influences people who do not recognize him as Scottish, are we justified in talking of Scottish influence? Few of the translations discussed here have any overt Scottish content: any national dimension must be supplied from the reader's background knowledge. A striking exception is the 1985 Japanese translation of Thomas Brown's *Church and State in Scotland*, a study (originally published in 1891) of the conflict over church establishment between the Church of Scotland and the Free Church following their split in 1843. As Professor Stewart J. Brown has suggested, this recondite work may have a live resonance for Japanese Christians anxious about their place in contemporary society.

So, the Scottish Enlightenment conception of progress poses interesting questions about the place of translation in modernity. It implies that all societies, however remote in space and time, exist within a single continuum, meaning that translation can provide a direct link between any two points. Translation can work in opposite directions here, either pointing us towards a common human nature that underlies superficial cultural differences or highlighting those very differences. By reflection it can offer us images of our own society as seen through the eyes of others. Equally, if the theory of stadial history is correct, translation can offer insights into our own culture at different times, future as well as past. But it also implies that, sooner or later, we are all headed for the same destination, a unified global culture. If so, what final role remains for translation?

Poetry

A C Clarke
Translating Paul-Jean Toulet

From *Les Contrerimes* (1921)

I

Avril, dont l'odeur nous augure
    Le renaissant plaisir,
Tu découvres de mon désir
    La secrète figure.

Ah, verse le myrte à Myrtil,
    L'iris à Desdémone:
Pour moi d'une rose anémone
    S'ouvre le noir pistil.

April, whose scent foretells
    reviving pleasure,
you show the secret face
    of my desire.

Ah, give Myrtilla myrtle,
    iris for Desdemon:
for me a pink anemone
    reveals her black pistil.

April, an' ah'm oot ma shell
oot ma heid wi' longin' –
a' they … smells.

Ah'm no' yin fur fancy flooers,
iris an' that
but a wee pink anemone
hir sex showin'.

II

Toi qu'empourprait l'âtre d'hiver
   Comme une rouge nue
Où déjà te dessinait nue
   L'arôme de ta chair;

Ni vous, dont l'image ancienne
   Captive encore mon cœur,
Ile voilée, ombres en fleurs,
   Nuit océanienne;

Non plus ton parfum, violier,
   Sous la main qui t'arrose,
Ne valent la brûlante rose
   Que midi fait plier.

You, who in winter firelight
   glowed like a rosy cloud
your body's scent already
   telling me you were nude;

island whose cloud-veiled image
   long since enchanted me,
shaded groves in blossom,
   nights of a southern sea;

sweet stock, whose fragrance grows
   with watering: not one
is worth the burning rose
   which bows her head at noon.

Nae use gangin' on aboot lang syne
the lassie wi' hir skin aw glowin
in fire-licht (ah knew she wis nakit
jist the smell o' hir)
thon island ah kent lang syne,
ah'll niver forget the flooers
an' clouds …

See, they wis aw fine an' weel
but no a patch on this yin,
ma burnin' rose
that hangs hir heid in the sun.

III

Iris, à son brillant mouchoir
  De sept feux illumine
La molle averse qui chemine,
  Harmonieuse à choir.

Ah, sur les roses de l'été,
  Sois la mouvante robe,
Molle averse, qui me dérobe
  Leur aride beauté.

Et vous, dont le rire joyeux
  M'a caché tant d'alarmes,
Puissé-je voir enfin des larmes
  Monter jusqu'à vos yeux.

In seven skybright colours
  a shining rainbow
glints through the gentle shower
  which falls timely, and slow.

Gentle shower, trail your hems
  to hide from me
the glare of summer roses,
  their arid beauty.

And you whose laugh disguises
  so many fears –
let me see in your eyes
  at last the hint of tears.

There's a rainbaw lichtin' up the sky
wi' hir seven colours, lichtin' up
the smirr that's takken the dust aff
simmer roses – awfu' bricht they are
an' a stang i' the ee, that wee bittie rain's
drawin' a veil.

Yis, an that gaes fur you,
wha's ay laughin', makkin'
as if ye didnae care 'boot anythin'
a'most, whan ah ken yer hert's
burstin' wi' fear. Ah'd lik fine
tae see yer greet.

IV

Ces roses pour moi destinées
   Par le choix de sa main
Aux premiers feux du lendemain
   Elles étaient fanées.

Avec les heures, un à un,
   Dans la vasque de cuivre,
Leur calice tinte et délivre
   Une âme à leur parfum

Liée, entre tant, ô Ménesse,
   Qu'à travers vos ébats,
J'écoute résonner tout bas
   Le glas de ma jeunesse.

She picked these roses out for me
   herself. They didn't last.
One by one, by dawn next day,
   they'd given up the ghost.

Each hour, in the copper bowl
   another drooped its head
like the chime of a clock; the soul
   locked in its perfume fled;

Just so, though charmed by all
   your blandishments, you wanton,
I hear my youth's death-knell
   tolling deep down.

Thon roses – she picked oot
ivry last yin, onie yisterday.
They're near deid jist the same.

Yin by yin they're losin'
thir smell, heids droopin'
on the hour, lik they wis clocks.
Ah'm nae different –

ye kin dae ivrything ye kin think uv
tae mak me forget –
ah'm still hearin' the bell
that says "yer best years is gane."

V

Dans le lit vaste et dévasté	I wake, touch her gently,
J'ouvre les yeux près d'elle;	in the vast, rumpled bed;
Je l'effleure: un songe infidèle	she's tight in a dream's hold,
L'embrasse à mon côté.	betraying me.

Dans le lit vaste et dévasté
   J'ouvre les yeux près d'elle;
Je l'effleure: un songe infidèle
   L'embrasse à mon côté.

Une lueur tranchante et mince
   Échancre mon plafond.
Très loin, sur le pavé profond,
   J'entends un seau qui grince...

I wake, touch her gently,
   in the vast, rumpled bed;
she's tight in a dream's hold,
   betraying me.

A narrow gleam of light
   splinters the ceiling.
Far down I hear a bucket
   scrape the pavement ...

Openin' ma een in the mussed bed
ah gies hir a nudge. No' a peep
oot hir, a dream's sae deep in hir
it's indecent – an' she's richt next me, but.

A skelf o' licht's prickin' the ceiling.
Ah hear a pail
doun on the pavement, skreekin'.

VI

Il pleuvait. Les tristes étoiles
   Semblaient pleurer d'ennui.
Comme une épée, à la minuit,
   Tu sautas hors des toiles.

It was a wet night. The dreary stars
   seemed bored to tears. The hour
chimed twelve. You leapt from the sheets
   quick as a rapier.

– Minuit! Trouverai-je une auto,
   Par ce temps? Et *le pire*,
C'est mon mari. Que va-t-il dire,
   Lui qui rentre si tôt?

'Midnight! Will I find a taxi
   at this time of night?
Worse still, what will *he* say
   when I get back late?'

– Et s'il vous voyait sans chemise,
   – Vous, toute sa moitié?
– Ne jouez donc pas la pitié.
   – Pourquoi? Doublons la mise.

'If he saw you now what would *he say*
   – his better half stark naked?'
'Don't play the pity card'
   'Why not? Let's up the stakes.'

It wis pissin' doun rain. The stars thirselves
wis greetin' wi' boredom. Twelve!
Ye skipit oot the bed
lik ye wis on hot coals,
"Whaur'll ah fin' a taxi at midnight?
An what'll ma man say?"

"What'd he say if he wis here
in this room? An' you bare-nakit?"
"Ach! Dinnae pretend tae be sorry fur him!"
"Whit fur no'? Ups the ante."

Sarah Paterson
Translating Six Māori Songs from her Childhood into her Father's Language

Bagpipe Waiata

Hine e Hine

E tangi ana koe	You are weeping
Hine e hine	Little girl, darling girl
E ngenge ana koe	You are weary
Hine e hine	Little girl, darling girl
Kati tō pōuri rā	Be sad no longer
Noho i te aroha	There is love for you
Te ngākau o te Matua	In the heart of the Father
Hine e hine	Little girl, darling girl

Ye're greetin' tae yersel
Wee lass, oh ma gurl
Forfochtan, like masel
Wee lass, oh ma gurl

Ken nae more the douth
O' lo'e ye'll aye hae routh
I th' hert o' God yir faither
Wee lass, oh ma gurl.

Te Rauparaha's Haka

Ka mate! Ka mate! Ka ora! Ka ora!
Ka mate! Ka mate! Ka ora! Ka ora!
Tēnei te tangata pūhuruhuru
Nāna nei i tiki mai, whakawhiti te rā
A upane! ka upane!
A upane! ka upane!
Whiti te rā! Hi!!

'Tis death, 'tis death! 'Tis life, 'tis life!
'Tis death, 'tis death! 'Tis life, 'tis life!
This is the man, covered in hair
Who has made the sun shine
Higher, and higher
Higher, and higher
The Sun shines!!

It's deith, it's deith! It's lyf, it's lyf!
It's deith, it's deith! It's lyf, it's lyf!
This is yer man, hairy, strang, pretty
Wha maks the sun skire
Heich, heichmaist
Heich, heichmaist.
The sun glent!

Now is the Hour

Pō atarau	On a moonlight night
E moea iho nei	I see in a dream
E haere ana	You going away
Koe ki pāmamao	To a distant land
Haere rā	Farewell
Ka hoki mai anō	But return again
Ki i te tau	To your loved one,
E tangi atu nei	Weeping here

Moonlicht nicht
Ah see 'na dream
Ye're gaun awa
Tae some hyne place.

Fare ye weel
But return aince mair
Tae yir ain belov'd
Wha's greetin hereawa

Pōkarekare Ana

Pōkarekare ana
ngā wai o Waiapu,
Whiti atu koe hine
marino ana e.

They are agitated
the waters of Waiapu,
But when you cross over girl
they will be calm.

E hine e
hoki mai ra.
Ka mate ahau
I te aroha e.

Oh girl
return to me,
I could die
of love for you.

They are fykit hereawa,
Thi lochs an watters o this laund
But, ma gurl, if ye gang ower
They'll be lown as onything

Oh my ain lass,
Come hame tae me
Ah'm weedin' awa
Fir love o' ye

One Day a Taniwha

Tētahi taniwha	One day a taniwha
Kauhoe i te moana	Went swimming in the moana
Kōhimu i tāku taringa	He whispered in my taringa
"Kia haere tāua	"Won't you come along with me
Tipi haere tirotiro	There such a lot to see
I raro i te moana."	Underneath the deep blue sea."
Ka mea au "Kāo, kāo, kāo!	I said "Oh, no, no, no!
Me haere, haere koe	You'd better go, go, go,
Ahakoa he hoa tāua.	Although I know we could be friends.
Tatari ana tāku Māmā	My Mama's waiting for me
Kei raro i te rākau kōwhai	Underneath the kowhai tree
Taniwha, haere rā."	Taniwha, haere rā!"

The Loch Ness Monster, she
Met me in her loch the day
She speirit in ma lug tae me
Will ye no come wi me
Thare's sic a heap tae see
Aneath ma bonnie loch wi me

Ah said "Ach na, na, na
Ye'd better gang awa, awa, awa
E'en though we could'a been pals.
Ma mammie bides fir me
Aneath an alder tree
So fare ye weel, Nessie, fare ye weel!"

E Minaka Ana

E minaka ana taku waha
Ki te kai a te rangatira,
Tāku reo rangatira
Tāku kuru pounamu tuku iho.

I desire that
my talk be like that of a leader,
my noble language
my precious inheritance.

Mīharo kē ana
Ki tōna pakari kia ora
Tē memeha, te wairua
ki te kōrero Māori

Astound me
with your maturity by
the evanescence, the spirit you show
when speaking Māori.

Kia kaha tātou
Ki te kōrero Māori!

Let us be staunch
in speaking Māori!

Ah want ma patter tae be
Lyk a noble chieftain or a dacent MP
Ma sacred livin langwij,
Ma great heirship from ma forebeirs an aw

Dumfoond me wi yir mense
an aw thi spirit that ye kythe when ye speak wi me.
Speakin in thi leid o Scots
Ye show yir pride and lair for yir history.

Binna feart, be stainch an leal
Keep speakin Scots for aye!!

Christine De Luca
Translating Nordic Poetry

From *In Hús eru aldrei ein* / *Black Sky* (2011) by Aðalsteinn Ásberg
Sigurðsson (Icelandic & English); Shetlandic by Christine De Luca

Tregahiminn   **Black Sky**

Blakkur himinn og hnúkur   Black skies and a mountain
fjalls yfir djúpum dali.   peak over a deep valley.

Atburðir hverfa í gleymsku   Events vanish into oblivion
andrá milli lífs og dauða.   instants between life and death.

Tunglið þokast um þumlung   The moon advancing by an inch
tíminn mjakast fram.   time is wearing on.

Black Lift

Black lift an gnarled
felly-heichts owre a deep daal.

Happenins mizzle awa inta naethin
blinks atween life an daeth

Da mön inchin peerie-wyes
time is wearin on.

Hrossagaukur

Nú ert þú einn eftir og þið fuglarnir
getið haft alla ykkar hentisemi
þótt húsið sé ef til vill ekki lengur
eftirsóknarvert til hreiðurgerðar.
Ungarnir þurfa ekki að óttast
óvæginn ljáinn í slyngri sláttuvél
og geta rölt óhræddir um túnið
sem óðum þýfgast að nýju.
Ó já, hrossagaukur, láttu nú bresta á
með hlátri og sköllum
sem fylla loftið af lífi og þrá.

Snipe

Now you are left alone and you birds
can do as you see fit
though the house is maybe no longer
desirable for a nest.
The young don't have to fear
the deft mower's ruthless blade
and can ramble unafraid in the meadow
which is fast turning bumpy again.
Oh yes, snipe, now you should burst out
into laughter and shouting
that fills the air with life and longing.

Horsegock

Noo you're aa your lane an you föls
can plaese yoursels
though da hoose is maybe
hardly kirsen for your nest noo.
Da laachter needna be faert
o da maaer's haertless sye, his vynd,
can skrovvel faerless i da mödow
dat, afore wir een, is gyaain ta kyo.
O ya, horsegock, noo du sood burst oot
in galders an skirls
dat fills da lift wi life an virmishin.

From *kjensla av at det ikkje regnar andre stader enn her* (2004) by Øystein
Orten (Norwegian); English by Hilde Petra Brungot; Shetlandic by
Christine De Luca

19
du går til kyrkja
ein enkekledd morgon

orgelmusikk lyttar
om nokon er i salen

flokkar av namnlause reiser seg
og rasar saman mellom benkeradene

utrivne tunger påkallar underet
med tyske koralar

kyrkja er ein nedlagd kafé
oblaten mellom leppene ei krone på ein jukebox

folk gamle som krossfestingar
formar andleta til song

19
you go to church
a morning dressed in a widow's garments

organ music is listening
to find if anybody might be in the hall

crowds of nameless rise
and fall apart between the pews

extracted tongues call for the miracle
by means of German hymns

the church is a closed down café
the wafer between the lips one krone on a jukebox

people as old as crucifixions
shape their faces for the singing

19
du gengs tae da kirk
a moarnin riggit ithin weedow's plaags

organ music is löin
ta fin if der onyboady dere

mirds o da nameless raise dem
an faa sindry atween da pews

outrekkit tongues plöt for a miracle
trowe da psalm's harmony

da kirk is a vod café
sained lof atween da lips wan coin i da jukebox

fock aald as crucifixions
shape der faces for da sang

From *Painoton tila* (1998) by Riina Katajavuori (Finnish); English by
Herbert Lomas; Shetlandic by Christine De Luca

Lumen valo	Snowlight
Aion pitää puheen	I'll give a speech
jota säestää urkujen	accompanied by the organ
vaimea pauhu lehteriltä.	roaring softly from the loft.
Kaikki kuuntelevat,	They'll all be listening,
silmäpareista tunnistan	but I'll acknowledge
vain yhden.	only a single pair of eyes.
Tämä on talviuni	This is a winter dream,
hitaan verenkierron	the snowed-in cavern
luminen luola.	of a slow circulation.
Kuinka enkeli voisi	How could an angel's wing
säveltää sulkasiivillään,	feather-pen her song,
kun nuottipaperia hallitsee	when the music sheet's ruled
ahdas viivasto?	by narrow lines?
Kotikaupunkini on valkoinen tähti.	My home city's a white star.
Kävelen sen kuorrutetuilla kaduilla	I walk its icing streets –
kuin ulappani rannoilla.	coasting the city-shores.
En ole nähnyt susiemon nisiä	I've not glimpsed the
	she-wolf's dug
en maailman solisluita.	nor the world's collarbone.
Levyssä on naarmu, joka toistaa	A scratch on the record sticks at
kuinka kauan tätä oikein kestää.	'How long can this go on?'
Elämä pitkä, ei ulotu.	Long life, no longer.
Valitse oikeauskoisuus,	Choose the right belief,
minä uskon tyhjyyteen,	I believe in emptiness,
se ei ole sairaus	that's no malady

Snaalicht

A'll mak a speech
wi da organ brölin

saaftly fae da laft.
Dey'll aa be harkenin,

but A'll anse only
ta wan pair o een.

Dis a winter draem,
büried i da moorie

whaar braeth slows.
Foo can a angel's pens

scrieve her winged sang,
whan da music sheet's ruled

wi nairrow lines?
Mi hame toon's a whicht starn.

I crump hits icin streets –
traekin da cecty-shörmal.

A'm no glisked da hund's nooky
nor da aert's shooder-blade.

Da record sticks whaar hit's scordit at
foo lang can dis geng on?

Lang life, nae langer.
Wael da richt belief,

I believe in emptiness
dat's no a distress

From *Hegrehøyden* (2002) by Thor Sørheim (Norwegian); English by
John Irons; Shetlandic by Christine De Luca

Hegrehøyden

I toppen av svartortrærne vaier reirene
som mørke soler, på kanten sitter hegrehannen
skarp som en dolk og vokter røtter og mus
som kryper ned i sumpen, mosen som kravler
rundt på stammer og stein, det er tidlig
i mars, og brått folder vingene seg ut av reiret,

hese skrik knirker som morkne trær, det lukter
myrvann, fugleskitt og frosk, hegren fikserer
farene på bunnen av skogen, det er ennå så tidlig
i historien at et skrik gir mening
for dem som vokter eggene bare noen meter
fra bilene som skifter strategi to ganger i året,

og når hegrene forlater reirene i april
for å stå stille i sivet før de hugger etter fisken
har de fremdeles hegrehøyden inne, stedet
hvor livet begynner hest og hemmelig,
med overblikk over fangsten
og visshet om at faren aldri er over.

Heron Heights

In the tops of the black alder trees the nests sway
like dark suns, on the edge sits the male heron
sharp as a dagger, keeping a watchful eye on rats and mice
creeping below in the marsh, the moss that crawls
over tree-trunks and stones, it is early
March, and suddenly wings unfold from the nest,

hoarse screeches creak like rotten trees, there is a smell
of bogwater, bird droppings and frogs, the heron gazes
fixedly at the dangers on the forest floor, it is still
so early on yet that a screech makes sense
for those guarding the eggs just a few metres
from the cars that change strategy twice a year,

and when the herons leave the nest in April
to stand motionless in the reeds before lunging for fish
they still have the heron heights close by, the place
where life begins hoarsely and secretly,
with a bird's-eye view of the catch
and the certainty that danger is never over.

Hegri-Heichts

I da taps o da black alder trees da nests sway
lik dark suns, apö da aedge da male hegri
shairp as a dagger an skoitin for rats and mice
skrovvellin doon i da dub, da moss dat arls
owre tree-trunks an steyns, hit's aerly
Mairch, an in a stowen dunt wings unfaald fae da nest,

haerse screchs crex lik rotten trees, der a waff
o miry watter, bird-scoot an frogs, da hegri skiles
da dangers apö da forest flör, hit's still sae aerly
i da story dat a screch hadds meanin
for dem guardin da eggs barely a yard or twa
fae tracks haevy wi daddery o voar tractors,

an whan da hegries laeve da nest in April
ta staand stock-still i da reeds afore stabbin eftir fish
dey still hae da hegri-heichts in-by, da place
whaar life sterts oot haerse an hiddlt awa,
wi a bird's-eye view o da catch
an da certainty dat danger is nivver owre.

Jennifer Williams
Translating Haris Psarras

Flourishing Lie

Methodically,
I notice the garden
fragmented
in wet eyes.

I cut my branch,
hear laughter
or the alleged shout
of a flower.

The more I penetrate
spring, the more I am overcome
by a verdant snowflake,
an obstacle to sowing.

Το ψέμα καταπράσινο

Μεθοδικά με μάτια υγρά
τον κήπο αντιλήφθηκα
και κάτοπτρο τα δάκρυα.

Κόβω το πρώτο μου κλαδί
ακούω γέλιου ζύμωση
ή κλάμα τάχα από
λουλούδι ανεξιχνίαστο.

Όσο εισχωρώ στην άνοιξη
τόσο μ' αφήνει πίσω
το ρίγος το χειμέριο
που μ' έφερε ως εδώ
νιφάδα χλοερή σποράς εμπόδιο.

Cloud Seeding

A craftsman with a poor name
slips and falls in the wind.
His fame, a hermetic stone,
advises Aeolus:

"Enunciate my voice,
make it heard by waves
rising, promising time's
condescension before too late.

A warm re-hearing, a hammer's sound.
And let them call me
flowers' pollen, spread all over the place or
the artificial rain that everyone deserves."

Τεχνητή βροχή

Τεχνίτης μ' όνομα φτωχό
γλιστρά και σπάει στον άνεμο
η φήμη του πέτρα κλειστή
τον άνεμο προτρέπει.
Πες τη φωνή μου καθαρά
σε όσους είναι κύματα
κι ορθώνονται για να βιαστεί
του χρόνου η συγκατάβαση.
Αναφηλάφηση ζεστή
πλάι στου σφυριού τον ήχο
κι άσε να με εκλάβουνε
ως γύρη απανταχού
παρούσα γύρη τεχνητή
βροχή που τους αξίζει.

Cicada

Take a breath and keep quiet.

The scale is more than your song.
Extension expires. Summer has gone
toward the seaweed on the shore.

Take a deep breath and spit out
all investment the sun made in you.

Nightingales, musicians, bells
have luxuriated in melody.

Your own sound is instantaneous,
a sign of warmth that fades.

Day comes to an end.
The beach closes
for the end of the season.

Go silent now and breathe.

Return to your body. Notice
your crackling steel wings.
Your fragile heel is freezing.
Your antenna that once was sharp, sky-reaching,
declines and nullifies
your brave shadow, cicada.

Ο τζίτζικας

Ανάπνεε τζίτζικα και πάψε
την κλίμακα δεν ανεβαίνει το τραγούδι σου
εκπνέει η παράταση και πάει το καλοκαίρι
πάει προς τα φύκια και τις αποβάθρες.
Πάρε βαθειά εισπνοή και φτύσε
όσα επένδυσε σε σένα ο ήλιος, τζίτζικα
ανάπνεε ασύμμετρα και τρέχα
από 'δω παν κι άλλοι.
Αηδόνια, καμπανούλες, μουσουργοί
εντρύφησαν στους ήχους για καιρό
ο θόρυβός σου είναι θόρυβος στιγμής
σύμβολο μιας θερμότητας που σβήνει
στη σμίκρυνση της μέρας και μαδά
κατάκοιτα τα τόσα παγωτά
στο γύφο η αμμουδιά κι η παραλία
σώπασε πια κι ανάπνεε
γύρνα στο σώμα σου και κοίτα
τα ατσάλινα φτερά πώς κροταλίζουν
παγώνει η ευαίσθητη η φτέρνα στο κλαδί
κι άκου καλά κυρίως την κεραία σου
που ήταν αιχμηρή ψηλά στα μάτια κορυφή
ήταν η κεραία σου
και τώρα πέφτει και ξεπέφτει
και καταργεί το θαρραλέο σχήμα σου
πέφτοντας η κεραία, τζίτζικά μου.

Forecasting the Weather

Fifteen leagues under clouds —
the circumnavigation of earth.
Running round in circles
a beautiful lady makes us bleed and the wind

places his breath on soil, his last one.
Take it as it comes.
The perfect shape has always been
the shape of the end.

It shines on the horizon
with rubies, emeralds and sunlight.
It shines and cuts the links that keep us together.
A crowd of clouds,

cloudiness. It's just your heart knows
the rain. As it runs from one room
to another, the rain has no end,
ends up your friend.

Μετρώντας τον καιρό

Δεκαπέντε λεύγες κάτω από τα σύννεφα
ο περίπλους της γης
φέρνει κύκλους
μια όμορφη
μας ματώνει

και στο χώμα ο άνεμος την πνοή του αφήνει
την τελευταία του πνοή
έτσι έχουν τα πράγματα, λες
το τέλειο σχήμα ήταν πάντοτε
το σχήμα του τέλους

λάμπει στον ορίζοντα
όλο πετράδια και φως και ήλιο
λάμπει και κόβει τους δεσμούς
που μας κρατούν οικείους
συννέφων πλήθος συννεφιά

μόνο η καρδούλα μου το ξέρει
πως τρέχει μες στο σπίτι μια
βροχούλα δίχως τελειωμό
βροχή που σε κερδίζει.

White Night

Streets narrow. Snow piles up.
Inevitable laws, the natural ones.

Tough, even ruthless.
From time to time, fair and mild.

Life remains unaltered.
Legislators try transformation, as snow does

when it changes your mood, when it encircles
with white

one who's alone,
losing his way back home.

Λευκή νύχτα

Έκλεισε απόψε το χιόνι τους δρόμους.
Έχει η ζωή δικούς της νόμους.

Σκληροί κι αμείλικτοι ενίοτε φαντάζουν
άλλοτε πάλι μοιάζουν δίκαιοι κι ορθοί.

Χάρη σ' αυτούς μένει απαράλλαχτη η ζωή
μα αγάλι αγάλι οι νομοθέτες δοκιμάζουν

να την αλλάζουν προς στιγμήν, όπως το χιόνι
τη διάθεσή μου αλλάζει σαν κυκλώνει

μ' άσπρες νιφάδες εκείνους που
τον δρόμο χάσανε του γυρισμού.

Eucalyptus

The eucalyptus is not undulating.
In the back yard a football remains
stagnant as a sleeping beauty.

It is black. And white.
It is blooming.
Children grew up.

The dormant memory
resembles a broken gun's bullet.
Spring waters it with the willow's tears.

Ο ευκάλυπτος δεν κυματίζει

Ο ευκάλυπτος δεν κυματίζει
και στην αυλίτσα μένει
στάσιμη σαν κοιμωμένη
μαύρη λευκή κι ανθίζει

μια μπάλα ποδοσφαίρου
παρατημένη βιαστικά
πώς μεγαλώσαν τα παιδιά
θραύσμα ταχύ ασφαίρου

περιστρόφου μοιάζει
η αδρανής ανάμνηση
στο σχήμα της το σφαιρικό η άνοιξη
δάκρυ κλαιούσης στάζει.

Donald Adamson
Translating Eeva Kilpi

from *Voices from an Old People's Home* (1996)

Today I've felt surprisingly well –
and oh how I wish…

That I could walk freely again,
pull a shopping trolley behind me,
lean on a tree sometimes.
That the dark days of October would return –
evenings when the wind is whistling, the last leaves flying
and he would dare to visit me
and no one would see him from behind the curtains.
That the morning would come
and it would be half past ten
and he'd phone.
And he'd say: Let's go for a drive, it's a fine day.
And we'd drive and look for a dry spot among the cliffs,
or a deserted house or a broken-down barn
or an old dance pavilion
      where suddenly
      greatly daring
      we could
      like when we were young…

Once when I was leaning on a tree
someone came by and said: Can I help you?
– No, I said, no thanks,
I have to manage on my own.

There's your rival, my dear. Old age.

• • •

Tänään olen voinut kummallisen hyvin
ja miten kaihoankaan.

Että saisi vielä kerran kulkea vapaana,
vetää ostoskärryjä perässään,
nojata välillä puuhun.
Että tulisivat lokakuun märät pimeät
viuhuvat illat, viimeisten lehtien lento
ja hän uskaltaisi tulla
eikä kukaan näkisi häntä verhojen raosta.
Että tulisi aamu
ja kello puoli yksitoista
ja hän soittaisi.
Sanoisi: – Lähdetäänkö ajelulle, on kaunis ilma.
Ja me ajelisimme etsien kuivaa kallionkoloa,
autiota taloa, romahtanutta latoa
tai vanhaa tanssilavaa
        jossa voisimme äkkiä
        uhkarohkeasti
        niin kuin nuorena...

Kerran kun nojasin puuhun
tuli joku sanomaan: – Voinko auttaa?
– Ei, minä sanoin, ei kiitos,
on jaksettava yksin.

Sinun kilpailijasi, rakkaani, on vanhuus.

Pain is my spouse
I shall not want.
He follows me to the green pastures,
watches over me when I try to rest
and even beside the restoring waters
he engraves me.
Though I anoint my body with oil
the cup of my pain is overflowing.
Pain is my Lord and my Shepherd
and I shall loll around in His mansions
till the end of my days.

The third in these patterns of love and death
is life.

Did you know that my dear?

_____

– You say it's dementia?
And that it's progressing?
That's not true.
I was absent-minded even when I was young,
I forgot things and it didn't bother me at all.
Quite the opposite. A lot of worries vanished from daily life
and I had less on my mind.
And nowadays, too, I forget things, I admit it.
But I can still remember
that I forget.

Kipu on minun puolisoni,
ei minulta mitään puutu.
Viheriäisille niityille hän minua seuraa,
valvoo minun yrittäessäni levätä,
virvoittavien vetten tykönäkin
hän minua kovertaa.
Vaikka voitelisin ruumiini öljyllä,
on kipujeni malja ylitsevuotavainen.
Kipu on minun Herrani ja Paimeneni
ja minä saan loikoa hänen huoneissaan
päivieni loppuun asti.

Se kolmas näissä rakkauden ja kuoleman kuvioissa,
se on elämä.

Tiesitkö sen, armaani?

_____

— Ai ettäkö dementiaa?
Ja että se etenee?
Ei pidä paikkaansa.
Jo nuorena minä olin hajamielinen,
unohtelin asioita eikä se vaivannut minua yhtään.
Päinvastoin. Moni huoli putosi pois päiväjärjestyksestä
ja mieleni keveni.
Myös nykyään minä unohdan asioita, myönnän sen.
Mutta yhä muistan
että unohdan.

So he's dead now,
my former husband,
a beautiful man.

All you women who got to enjoy him,
why don't you show your gratitude now,
and your respect for him?
Why didn't you show it when he was alive?
Why were you the first to condemn him,
declaring our marriage an empty shell?
Why did you point the finger at him
when his bad conscience drove him to drink
and he screamed at us at home?
Why didn't you support him even for your own sakes?
Why didn't you clean his floor
of vomit and shit?
Why were none of you a mother, sister
or nurse for him? An aunt. A teacher.
Yes – really – why weren't you?

He was a man for all women
and you used him.
Though so did I.

And here we stand, the ones left, survivors.

• • •

That was true love.
When I farted he said:
– How beautiful!

Hän on nyt kuollut,
minun entinen mieheni,
kaunis mies.

Kaikki te naiset jotka saitte nauttia hänestä,
miksi ette nyt osoita kiitollisuuttanne
ja kunnioitustanne hänelle?
Miksi ette osoittaneet sitä jo hänen eläessään?
Miksi olitte ensimmäisinä häntä tuomitsemassa,
julistamassa meidän avioliittomme pintapuolisuutta?
Miksi osoititte häntä sormellanne
kun hän huonoon omaantuntoonsa joi
ja rähjäsi meille kotona?
Miksi ette tukeneet häntä edes itsenne tähden?
Miksi ette siivonneet hänen lattioitaan
kun hän oksensi, ulosti?
Miksi kukaan ei ollut hänelle äiti, sisar,
huolehtija? Täti. Opettaja.
Niin todellakin: miksi?

Hän oli yleinen mies
ja te käytitte häntä hyväksenne.
Vaikka niinhän tein minäkin.

Tässä seisomme jäljellä, selviytyjät.

• • •

Oli se rakkautta.
Kun minulta pääsi pieru
hän sanoi:
– Miten kaunista!

My dear, at a certain stage
there will be a change of tense,
in fact it has already changed
without our noticing it
and whatever happens
has already happened
long ago
and will never happen again.
There is no past
that will return
and no future
that we rush towards,
that pulls us into its vortex –
only this moment
not bound to anything.
Do you know what it's called?

Yesterday they said on TV
that it's Alzheimer's Disease.

I hear the cry of the cranes.
At this time of year they fly to the south.
That much I remember.

I hear the cries of the children in the meadow
from the open window.
Children grow up quickly.
That too I remember.

Jossain vaiheessa
aikamuoto muuttuu, rakkaani,
on jo muuttunut,
huomaamattamme,
ja mikä tapahtuu
on jo tapahtunut
kauan sitten
eikä enää toistu.
Ei ole menneisyyttä
joka palaa,
ei tulevaisuutta
joka kiitää kohti
ja tempaa meidät pyörteeseensä,
on vain tämä hetki
ilman siteitä.
Tiedätkö mikä se on nimeltään?

Eilen sanottiin televisiossa
että se on Alzheimerin tauti.

Kuulen kuinka kurjet huutavat.
Ne lentävät tähän aikaan kohti etelää.
Sen verran muistan.

Kuulen lasten huudot niityltä
avoimesta ikkunasta.
Lapset kasvavat nopeasti.
Myös sen muistan.

You wake up in the morning and you hope
that your old age would have evaporated during the night.
In your sleep you've forgotten that you are old.
And sick.
You think that in the night you'll get better
and wake up healthy.
As it was with father on his deathbed. And mother.
But they had to wake up in order to be dying.
I remember that feeling.
We shared it.

• • •

I like people who have an open mind:
people who are able to say: Yes?
Really? Well, well, I didn't know.
I hadn't thought of that.

An open mind is more than wisdom,
more than being right,
more than "What did I tell you?" or
"I've known that ever since…"

• • •

Are you saying I didn't praise you
enough?

But who would praise their own flesh and blood,
it would be like praising oneself.

And why didn't anyone tell me:
You are the most important person in the world to your child,
nothing can replace you!

Sitä herää aamulla ja toivoo
että vanhuus olisi yön aikana haihtunut.
Nukkuessaan on unohtanut olevansa vanha.
Ja sairas.
Odottaa että yön aikana parantuisi
ja heräisi terveenä.
Niin isäkin kuolinvuoteellaan. Ja äiti.
Mutta oli herättävä tekemään kuolemaa.
Muistan sen tunteen.
Me jaoimme sen.

• • •

Minä pidän ihmisistä joilla on avoin mieli.
Ihmisistä jotka pystyvät sanomaan: Ai?
Niinkö? Vai niin. En tiennytkään.
Tuota en ole tullut ajatelleeksi.

Avoin mieli on enemmän kuin viisaus,
enemmän kuin oikeassa oleminen,
enemmän kuin "johan minä sanoin" ja
"minä tiesin sen jo vuonna…"

• • •

Ai että minä en kehunut teitä
tarpeeksi?

Kuka nyt omaa lihaansa ja vertansa,
sehän olisi kuin olisi kehunut itseään.

Entä miksi kukaan ei sanonut minulle:
Sinä olet lapsillesi kaikkein tärkein ihminen,
sinua ei korvaa mikään!

I look up
and there are leaves on the maple tree.

– I'm sorry
I tell my son
but could you be a little more
like a father to me?

• • •

The faults that desire to grow within people
seek out a mother to be born in.
It happens spontaneously
for everything must have a beginning.
The faults in my children
seek me
and your children's seek you.
and our own faults
seek our mother.

That's the way it is, boys.

Nostan katseeni
ja vaahterassa on lehdet.

– Minä pyydän anteeksi,
sanon pojalleni,
mutta voisit sinäkin olla
vähän isällisempi minua kohtaan.

. . .

Ne viat jotka ihmiseen haluavat kehittyä
etsivät synnyttäjäkseen äidin.
Etsimällä etsivät
sillä pitäähän kaikella alkunsa olla.
Minun lasteni viat
etsivät minut,
sinun lastesi sinut
ja meidän omat vikamme
meidän äidin.

Niin se on poijjaat.

Christopher Whyte
Translating Brian Johnstone

Cothan/Reliquary (2003)

Truinnean
nan iasg loinnreach
na cloich bàin
cnàmh a rinn
an Tighearna fhèin
a' cur an fhir seo
air ceann a chèile

Ninian
of the bright fish
the white stone
bone of the Lord's
own making
places this
one upon the other

Coluimcille
sgrìobhte dà uair
a' gabhail an fhacail
à fearann uaine
ga chur a' snàmh
ann an làimh
de gheugan 's de sheiche

Columba
twice written
takes the word
from a green land
floats it
in a hand
of branches and skin

Donnan
a' siubhal nan cnoc
a' gabhail na slighe cumhaing
nam bealaichean àrda
leabhar is bachall
a dheòin fhèin
clach is crois is uisge

Donan
the hill traveller
walks the narrow road
the high passes
book and staff
his own will
stone and cross and water

Faolan
solas san duibhre
'g òl uisg' à fuaran
na talmhainn fhèin
a' togail a ghàirdein
ris an fhacal
a tha soilleir sa chraiceann

Fillan
light in the darkness
drinks from the water
of earth's own spring
raises his arm
to the word
bright within the skin

Aodhan
nam briathran caoine
anail mhilis nam beathach
a' giùlan an leòis thuath
thar a' ghainmhich
thar na mòintich
an tìr dheas seo

Aidan
of the gentle words
of beasts' sweet breath
carries the north light
over sand
over marsh beds
this southern land

Caoibeart
beò ann an gaoir na faoileig
an iarmailt mhòr
briste le eileanan
a' leaghadh
salann an àile
grèim na gealaich

Cuthbert
alive in the gull's cry
the great sky
broken by islands
renders
the salt air
the moon's grip

Prose

Colin Donati
Translating Fyodor Dostoevsky

From *Crime and Punishment* (1866) Part 2, Chapter 1

Raskolnikov at the Polis

Sanct Petersburg in the swaltry simmer o 1865. The ex-student Raskolnikov, on the mornin efter cairryin oot the premeditated murder o a local pawnwife, is waukent in bumbazement in his attic lodgins – the fouty chaumer he canna afford to pey his rent on – by the unexpectit delivery o a summons to cry in at the local bureau o the polis for his side o the city. Forbye his confusion, and teeterin wi the onset o a fever, the young murderer walks oot in the switherin city heat to obey the fearfu summons…

Frae his bit to the polis was haurly a quarter verst. They had just flittit to new lodgins in a new tenement on the fourth flair. He had cried in at the auld bureau aince in the bygane, but lang syne. As he cam through the pend, he saw a peasant steppin oot frae a stair on the richt wi a filebook in his airms. "A jannie, I dout. Sae I dout that's the bureau." And wi that guess he stairted on up the stair. He didna want to speir ony questions.

"I'll gae in, drap to my knees and gie them the haill story…" he thocht as he speeled up to the fourth flair.

The stair was stey, narra and aa slaistered wi syndins. Aa the kitchens to aa the lands on aa fower flairs backit onto the stair wi their doors hingin open the lee lang day. That was how it was a gey steuch. Trailin back and forrit, up and doon, went janitors wi

89

filebooks in their airms, polis, and men and weimen generally on appeyntments. The door to the bureau was hingin open tae. He gaed in and stopped ben the lobby. Some peasants there were somewey staunin waitin. It was a gey scomfishin heat tae, and on tap o that, a scunnersome guff o new, ill-setten pent, ranshy wi ile, frae aff o the new-pentit chaumers was gaun richt up his neb. He bade a wee, then decided to gae ben to the next chaumer. Aa the chaumers were hamperit and laigh-ceiled. A terrible fyke drew him faurer ben again. Naebody peyed him ony heed. In this second chaumer sat a wheen o clairks screivin awa at desks, nae mony dressed muckle better than him: it looked a richt clanjamphry. He turnt to ane o them.

"What dae ye want?"

He showed the summons frae the bureau.

"Ye're a student?" speired the boy, keekin at the summons.

"Ay, ex-student."

The clairk gied him a quick scance, but wi nae particular interest. He was a gey towsie-haired loun wi a fixed thocht in his ee.

"I'll no learn ocht frae this ane; it's aa muckle aboot muckle to him," thocht Raskolnikov.

"In to the heid clairk," said the scribe, jaggin a fingre at the benmaist door.

He gaed in to a chaumer (the fourth ane ben) sma and packed ticht-fou wi folk, citizens better dressed a bit nor in the ither chaumers. There were twa weimen amang them. Ae wuman in murnin weeds, cheap anes, sat afore the heid clairk, at his desk, screivin to his dictation. The ither wuman by contrast gey bousome and purply-reid wi blebs, a kenspeckle wife, somewey overly grandly dressed, wi a brooch on her bosie the size o a flattie, stood for some reason waitin. Raskolnikov showed the heid clairk the summons. The boy took a quick keek, said "bide!" and cairried on dealin wi the wuman in murnin.

He breathed mair freely. "Sae it canna be yon onywey!" He was piece by piece findin hert again. He broddit himsell to hae mair smeddum and keep his guaird up.

"Ony daver, ony lack o thocht, and I could easy lat the haill cat oot o the bag! Hm... it could dae wi mair air in here," he gaed on,

"It's that stychly… my heid's gaun roon and roon… and my thinkin and aa…"

Aa inside him felt a terrible jurmummle. He was feart he wad loss the threid. He tried to cleek something, onything at aa wi nae connection, to think aboot, but just couldna dae it. He did hae a fell interest in the heid clairk, though: wanted aye to ettle at something in his face, to spy it. Fair a young laddie it was, twa-and-twenty year auld, wi features din and yare that gart him look aulder, dressed in a primpit and tip-o-the-new style, wi coos-lick hair slicked doun and pairted at the back, a bonny nummer o rings for his prinky white fingres, and gowd chines to his westkit. He even spoke a puckle words in French wi some furreign body that was there, and gey faisably tae.

"Louiza Ivaanovna, tak a seat," he said in the bygane to the vaudy purply-reid wife that stood like she didna daur sit, though a seat was in-aside her.

"*Ich danke*," she said, and wi a reeshle o silks, sat quaetly doon. Her licht-blue skirts wi pearlin o white filled oot like a balloon aroun her chair and took up just aboot hauf o the space o the bureau. There was a gey reek o perfume. The guidwife plainly took a beamer, though, at takkin up aa that space and giein oot sic waffs o scent. Her smile, baith creengin and crouse at the same time, plainly was ill-fashed.

The wuman in murnin finally feenished and stairted to rise. Aa at aince, in a kinna clatter, this gey swankie officer cam ben wi a swagger, sweein his shouders wi ilka step, drapped his toorie heckled cap on the table, and sat doon in a gairdy cheer. On seein him, the vaudy guidwife lowped up frae her place and stairted drappin curtchies wi a special rapture; but the officer didna pey ony heed and in his presence she didna daur sit doon again. He was a polis-luftenand, a helpender o the district maister, wi horizontal reid mustaches that stuck oot on baith sides, and gey nippie features that didna express muckle asides frae mebbe pride. He cast a kinna chawed and sidelangs glower at Raskolnikov: really it was shockin, the state o his claes; and yet for aa that, his ill-pitten-on look didna aye just haud wi his demeanour. Raskolnikov, taen aff his guaird, glowered back owre lang and direct, garrin him even tak the gee.

"What dae ye *want?*" he yelloched, likely frae the dumfooner that sic a minker hadna thocht to jouk the wulfire o his glower.

"I was bidden... I got a summons..." Raskolnikov managed somewey to say.

"It's yon case o the recovery o siller, frae the *student*," the heid clairk quickly pit in, ruggin himsell awa frae his papers. "Here, sir!" He pynted oot the place in a register and flung it owre to Raskolnikov. "Read!"

"Siller? What siller?" thocht Raskolnikov, "But... it canna be_yon onywey!" And he felt a sudden gliff o joy. His hert was a woner thing licht. It aa drapped frae his shouders.

"And what time daes it say ye were wantit, dear sir?" the luftenant fairly gollered, gettin himsell mair and mair raised somewey. "It says ye had to be here at nine, and it's noo the back o eleeven!"

"I just got it fifteen meenits syne," Raskolnikov answered back loodly owre his shouder, growin suddenly and surprisingly angert in return. He even took a pleisure in it. "It's a woner I'm here at aa, what wi this fever I'm comin doon wi."

"Kindly dinna goller!"

"I'm no gollerin, I'm just speakin. It's ye that's gollerin, but I'm a student and I'm no awa to let naebody goller at us."

Sae reid-radge the helpender was that he couldna say a word; for the first meenit it was aa just slavers fleein frae his mou. He lowped up frae the chair.

"Kindly haud yer *w-h-h-h-eesht!* Mind whaur ye are! Nae mair o yer *sc-r-r-r-aich*, sir!"

"Ay, and ye're in the same place yersell," cried Raskolnikov. "And, asides frae aa this goller, ye're smokin rollies wi nae thocht for the lave o us." Raskolnikov efter sayin this felt a selcouth cantiness.

The heid clairk was watchin wi a smile. The ramstam luftenant plainly was bumbazed.

"*That*, sir, is nane o yer *business!*" he cried in the end-up wi a yelloch that was past aa. "And ye will be sae *guid* as to mak oot the declaration demandit o ye. Shaw him, Alexander Grigorovitch. There's been complents! Ye dinna pey yer debts! See what a bricht spyrin merlioun we hae!"

But Raskolnikov wasna listenin ony mair, keenly gruppin the document and scansin it for answers. He read ainced, twiced, and didna unnerstaun.

"What's this?" he speired at the heid clairk.

"A bill o demand for ye to mak guid on a debt o siller ye owe. Either ye hae to pey in fou, wi aa costs, penalties, and siclike, or ye hae to mak oot a written libel statin whan it is ye'll can pey aa that's due, forbye giein a warrant that ye'll neither tak leg bail oot o the city, nor will sell, nor heel awa, nae guids nor gear for sae lang as the debt aye owes. And the creditor has freedom to sell ony gear ye hae and to bring against ye ony actions as accords in law."

"But I hinna… got ony debts!"

"That isna oor affair. We hae here an appeal for recovery on an ootstaunin and legally bindin bill o debt made oot by yersell nine month syne to the weedow o the college assessor Zarneitsyn for a hunner and fifteen rouble, made owre by this same weedow Zarneitsyn as peyable to the Coort Cooncillor Tchebarov, for the whilks ye hae been summonsed here to answer."

"But she's my lanlady!"

"What if she is?"

The heid clairk looked at him wi a couthy and ruefu smile, that had as weel a kinna triumph to it, as if at some greenhorn gettin it for the first time, as if to say, "Sae, what daes it feel like noo?" But what – what noo to him was ony letter o debt or bill for recovery! Was it worth the sweet noo, sic a thing as that – worth him peyin ony heed at aa! He stood, he read, he listened, he answered, he even speired questions o his ain, but it was aa meckanical. Joy at seein himsell safe, at haein won free frae pressin danger withoot comprisin, withoot gaun through the mull, withoot future ettlin or guessin, withoot doots, withoot questions, was aa that filled his hert at that meenit. It was a track o pure plain corporal pleisure. But at the same meenit, something like a brew o thunner and levin-licht was getherin in the bureau. The luftenand, still aa fraized at the shaw o disrespect, aa het up, and wantin, it was plain to see, to swage his hurt conceit o himsell, fell wi aa guns bleezin on the misfortunate "guidwife in grandery" that aa the time since his arrival had been gowkin at him wi the maist glaikit smile.

"And as for *ye*, ye – whatever-ye-are," he suddenly blastit at the tap o his lungs (the wuman in murnin was gane), what was that aa aboot last nicht, at your bit, eh? Mair deboshery and affront for the haill street to thole. Mair fechtin and drucken ongauns. Dae ye want the jyle! Did I no tell ye! Hae I no warned ye! Hoo efter the tenth time ye wadna be gettin aff wi it on the eleeventh. And here it's you again. *Again!* ye – whatever-ye-are!"

The document even drapped frae Raskolnikov's haun, and he cast a wild glower at the grand guidwife gettin sic short shrift. But he soon jaloused whit the case was aa aboot, and even stairted to enjoy it. Sic pleisure he got, listenin to it, that aa he wantit to dae was lauch and lauch and lauch… his nerves were lowpin.

"Ilya Pyetrovitch!" the heid clairk began tentily, but decided to haud fire; for really there was nae stoppin the ramstam luftenant just there and then ither than by main force – he kent that fine.

As for the guidwife in grandery, at the first hurl o thunner and fire-flaucht she took a glocken; but queer to say, the mair coorse and forcy his sweerin grew, the mair couthy and canty grew the smile she cast on the ramstam luftenant. She aye kept shauchlin and drappin curtchies whaur she stood, aye on hecklepins, til it was her turn to get a word in finally.

"At mines is nae cletter and fechts, Herr Kapiten," she aa at aince stairted to patter wi a strang German sooch like skailin peas, though her Russian was glibby eneugh, "and never, never it is shcandals, but drucken he kom, and I say aa, Herr Kapiten, and mines is nocht the vyte… the noble hoose I hae, Herr Kapiten, and the noble ongauns, Herr Kapiten, and ayvis, ayvis, never nae vye I vant shcandals. But drucken he kom, syne for tree pottles he speir, syne he lift up the foot and stairt for to play on the fortepianie vi the foot, and nae guid it is in a noble hoose, and *ganz* the fortepianie he brak, and never, never, nae vye it is guid menners, and I say. But he tak the pottle and awbody in the backs vi the pottle he pook. And here I stairt soon cries for the jannie, and Karl has kom, Karl he in the ee claff, and also Henrietta in the ee he claff, but me on the chook five times he claff, and in the noble hoose, Herr Kapiten, it is nae guid, and I skirl! Syne he unsteek to the canal the vindae and oink ootside the vindae like a soo, and it is wrang! Hoo can a body like the vee soo ootside the vindae skirl? Wrang it is! Ach ach ach! And Karl him frae ahint pou frae the vindae be the frok-coat and, Herr Kapiten, it is true, the frok-tail aa is rived, and he skirl hoo the man mun pey the fifteen rouble fine. And me mysell for *sein Rock*, Herr Kapiten, five rouble pey, and nae noble guest it is, Herr Kapiten, and he aavair mak shcandal! 'I vill,' he say, 'the muckle satire on ye *gedruckt*, for aboot ye I can scrieve in aa the newsblads aa I vant.'"

"Sae it was a writer, was it?"

"Aye, Herr Kapiten, and nae the noble guest at aa, Herr Kapiten, ven in a noble hoose..."

"Weel, weel, weel! That'll dae! If I hae telt ye afore, I hae telt ye a hunner times..."

"Ilya Pyetrovitch!" said the heid clairk again, wi meanin. The luftenant cast him a glower. The heid clairk gied a wee nod o the heid.

"Onywey, this is my last word to it, my esteemed *Laveeza* Ivaanovna, and I'm tellin ye, it's the *last*," the luftenant cairried on. "If ye hae ony mair ructions in that noble hoose o yours, even just ainced mair, it's *zugunder* ye'll get, to pit it doucely, ye hear me! Sae it was a writer was it? Some literary body in yer 'noble hoose' taks five roubles aff ye for his coat-tails, daes he? That's yer makars for ye!" And he cast a fleerin look at Raskolnikov. "Twa nichts syne in a supper-hoose there was anither ane just like it: taks his denner and disna want to pey, 'else I'll pit ye in a satire', says he. And anither ane tae on a steamship this ither week was miscaain a faimily o the tap gentry – a state cooncillor, his guidwife *and* his dochter – in the maist ill-faured language. And anither ane just the ither day gets himsell flung oot frae a pastie-shop. But that's the wey it is wi yer makars, yer screivers, yer students, yer toon-criers... Ach! Ye can gang! But I'll come keekin in bye soon eneugh... sae mind oot! Ye hear?"

The translator gives grateful thanks to Oleg Zubovich for useful commentary on the Russian original and to Ken Cockburn for advice on German elements.

Glossary and Notes

a gey steuch, a terrible stench
a puckle, a few
a wheen, a number
a woner thing, inexpressibly
ae, one
ainced owre, once over
ben, inside
benmaist, furthest in
blebs, blotches
body, person
bosie, bosom
bousome, buxom
brak, break
broddit, goaded
bumbazement, confusion
canty, pleasant
chawed, indignant
chines, chains
chook, cheek
claff, hit
clanjamphry, miscellaneous
collection (of people)
clatter, disturbance
comprisin, calculating
couthy, sympathetic
creengin, cowering
crouse, brazen
cry in, call by
curtchies, curtsies
daver, stupidity
din, dark (of face)
doucely, politely
drucken ongauns, drunken
behaviour
ettle at, discern
ettlin, 'riddling'
fell, considerable
flattie, saucer
fleerin, scornful
flittit, moved
forbye, in addition

fouty, derisory
fraized, amazed
fyke, restlessness
gairdy cheer, armchair
ganz (German), entire
gart him, caused him (to)
gaun through the mull, closely
analysing
gear, property
gedruckt (German), publish
gettin it, coming under fire
gey reek, strong scent
gey, very
glibby, smooth-tongued
gliff, moment
glocken, moment of fright
glower, look
goller, shout (outburst)
gowkin, staring
guidwife, respectable woman
hamperit, cramped
heel awa, conceal
helpender, (for помощник) aide
Ich danke, (German), I thank you
ile, oil
ill-aff, poor
ill-fashed, perturbed
ill-faured, impolite
ill-pitten-on, very unkempt
ill-setten pent, incorrectly
composed paint
in the bygane, incidentally
jannie (for дворник), caretaker
jouk, avoid (cringingly)
jurmummle, confusion
kenspeckle (for видная),
'distinguished'
laigh-ceiled, *adj.* having low
ceilings
lands, flats

lang syne, a long time ago
levin-licht, lightning
libel, formal letter
lowped, sprang
minker (for *оборванец*), ragamuffin
miscaain, slandering
mou, mouth
mun (maun), must
murnin-weeds, mourning-clothes
neb, nose
newsblads, newspapers
on hecklepins, on tenterhooks
past aa, beyond everything
pend (for *ворóта*), gated arch
piece by piece, little by little
polis, police
primpit, foppish
prinky, well-manicured
quarter verst (*Russian measure*),
  short distance equivalent to
  around a sixth of a mile
ramstam, unrestrained
ranshy, rank
reid-radge, violently angry
rived, torn
scance, scrutinizing glance
scomfishin, overpowering
scraich, shrill toned shout(ing)
screivin, writing
scunnersome guff, nauseating
  smell
sein Rock (*German*), his coat
selcouth cantiness, rare
  happiness
shauchlin, shuffling
side, district
siller, money
skailin, spilling
slaistered, wet

smeddum, inward strength
somewey, for some reason
soo, pig
sooch, timbre
speeled, climbed
speirin, asking
spy, 'get at'
spyrin merlioun, soaring falcon
stey (like 'sty'), steep
stychly, stuffy
sweein, swinging
sweet, anxiety
switherin, stifling
syndins, kitchen swill
tak leg bail, abscond
tak the gee, take offence
tentily, gaurdedly
that was how (for *оттогó*), that
  was why
the lave, the rest
tip-o-the-new, fashionable
took a beamer, showed
  embarrassment
toorie heckled cap, (for *фуражку*
  с кокардой) peaked helmet with
  cockade
track, spell
unsteek(it), open(ed)
vaudy, ostentatious
vyte (wyte), blame
waukent, awakened
westkit, waistcoat
wife, woman
wulfire, lightning
yare, eager
zugunder (*military expression*), the
  hundred

Donal McLaughlin
Translating Monica Cantieni

From *The Encyclopaedia of Good Reasons* (2011)

The narrator in Monica Cantieni's novel is a young girl, an immigrant to Switzerland whose adoption is still in the process of being finalized. Her new parents are Swiss (the father) and French, originally (the mother). The girl is learning German – the language spoken in her new community – and collects new words and phrases in word-boxes. The "voice" in this novel reflects the girl's at times not-quite-accurate use of newly-acquired language. Cantieni's use of a "limited perspective" also means that readers get to share the girl's (lack of) understanding of certain issues. The background to this extract is a referendum held in Switzerland in 1970 on the question of immigration.

Switzerland has plans. And one thing was sure – Eli wasn't part of the mix. Concrete was the one thing he got to mix. The wall he was looking up at was at an awkward stage, and his foreman was too. Eli had to get a move on. He was tugging impatiently at the plastic sheet he was spreading out on the ground.

– Go home.

– I can't.

– Porque? Why not?

At home, domestic bliss wasn't what it should be. The Peroxide Blonde said you could hear it down on the street even. Switzerland had plans that were totally upsetting my father. He was banging doors and my mother was going round after him, closing the

98

windows my father had just opened. This had been going on for days already.

– Why are they doing that?

Eli held a shovel out to me.

– Hold that.

– Go on, tell me.

– Because they're not of the same opinion.

– My father says Switzerland has plans.

– Plans? What kind of plans?

– *You*'ll have to explain that to me. The Peroxide Blonde won't tell me anything, says she doesn't understand *politics*. What's *politics*?

– I haven't time for that right now. As you can see.

He pointed at a pile of sacks of cement. Eli took one, swung it onto his back using just one hand – none of the other men could do that – and when he dropped it on the ground beside me, the sack burst, and we were standing in a cloud of dust that slowly settled again. Eli took the shovel back.

– What do you not look like?!

– What about *politics*?

– Give me peace with that. I've enough bother as it is.

– But it's important. Because of the *referendum*. What's a *referendum*? What's an *initiative*? And what's *foreign infiltration*? I'm not allowed to say that word at home, my father's already smashed the radio cos of it. Now we've no radio and our doors aren't going to last much longer, the Peroxide Blonde says. If we keep on like this, she says, the house will collapse too. My mother doesn't care though. She wants to drive off with me anyhow. Says she can't live with a marriage that's broken – and not with a *democracy* that's broken either. She can't even speak her mind at home. What's *democracy*, and what's *politics*?

You have to be stubborn if you want something in this country, Eli had said it himself, and especially if you're not sure you can stay. There's agreement across the world on this. Ask anyone who isn't a tourist but making a mad dash for another country cos, back home, they were scared shitless for as many different reasons as Oskar has hairs, Eli says. Him and his pals could tell you a thing or two about that, they could.

– But what about Switzerland, and what's *politics*?

Eli sighed. He made a hollow in the cement, put the shovel down and pulled me behind the toilet hut that was wobbling and flushing once a minute. It was their break.

– Switzerland is asking itself how many foreigners it wants to have here. Or, rather, James Schwarzenbach is asking the Swiss that. There are too many of us, Schwarzenbach reckons.

– Who is Schwarzenbach? They keep talking about him. Everyone does. My mother, Toni – and my father's nose goes white with rage if he even thinks of him. He says Schwarzenbach is completely destroying Switzerland and ruining his marriage. He says Schwarzenbach is a professional arsonist but makes out he's a fireman.

– He's a politician. He wants Switzerland to have a referendum on how many foreigners can be in Switzerland, how many of us can stay.

– What's *initiative*? And what's *foreign infiltration*?

– I've just told you.

– No, you haven't. And not *politics*, and not *democracy*.

– Your grandfather anyhow says, I've heard, that *democracy* isn't a question of taste or something you can use to make you yourself seem important, even if people like Schwarzenbach like to think so.

Eli looked to see where his foreman was. He bent down to the shovel, scratched a little dirt together, then mushed it in a puddle to make some browny-grey stuff. It was starting to rain. He put his collar up, put mine up too and brushed the wet hair out of my face.

– On you go home. I'll see you later.

There are words that the fattest encyclopaedia beside my bed tells you things about that tell you nothing. Experience teaches you that.

It was raining pasta and goulash sauce even before the plate hit the wall. My father was even more furious than the Housemother's dog used to get every time the postman who had once fed it barbed-wire sausage showed up. Something in the newspaper had enraged my father and my mother was working him up to livid. They had an *issue*.

Issue: something I wasn't asked about. ISSUE was in the future-words box. I didn't have an ISSUE yet. I merely was one, over and over again, just not at this moment. Right now, it's James Schwarzenbach, my father or my mother. Depending. It's *a matter of opinion*.

A matter of opinion: not an issue for me either.

Issues are words that foreigners have round their necks. – And what's far worse, my mother says, we have the foreigners round our necks cos there are so many now, with their suitcases from Italy. Word has spread about Switzerland, and my father says Schwarzenbach says that's the reason for the *foreign infiltration* here, *foreign infiltration* is the reason for his *initiative*, and because that was successful, there's now *The Referendum*. I phoned Tat so he could explain the words to me, but he didn't listen at all, just roared into the receiver that *initiatives* and *referenda* were gradually deteriorating into the favourite sports of *image-obsessed hooligans on the right*, and were also contributing to the Swiss expressing their views through the *ballot box*, instead of thinking first about *politics* and the *repercussions*. The rest of what he said, I couldn't understand. He hung up, no doubt cos his false teeth had fallen out again. I decided to think about *politics* immediately – as soon as someone could tell me what it was.

If my father could, he says, he'd run back and forward and vote as often as possible against this Schwarzenbach guy, who is to blame for everything – for my father having to shout, for him having to sleep for the past week on the sofa, for him not being able to sleep on the sofa, for him having to drink cos he's not allowed to sleep in his own bed, for him not being able to find the sofa cos he's been drinking, for him having to sleep on the kitchen floor and not being able to sleep there either, not for a minute.

– 1970! he roars through the kitchen. Don't ever forget 1970! This little son-of-an-industrialist. A millionaire, who claims to be one of us. Someone who has never lifted a finger, never had to work in his life, whose head it has never entered to work – someone like that's claiming to represent our interests. How can he know what they are? Come on, tell me! Cos if this twerp gets his proposal through, Eli and Toni will have to go home, Dejan and Mirela will have to go home, and you can stick your red-pepper relish and sheep's cheese

101

and milk bread and all the rest – three hundred thousand foreigners will go back to where they come from, will leave half-finished houses standing and streets dug up, will leave the kitchens, hotels, and launderettes where they work, the railway platforms, the foundries, the machine works. Schwarzenbach will be the ruin of them – he's destroying Switzerland, I swear. You don't need a degree to see that. Read up on what the guy wants, read it in his own rag.

My mother wanted to say something but my father roared he wasn't finished with her yet, and certainly not with Schwarzenbach.

– Him and his gang of sympathizers: look at them, they're opening their gobs now, think their chance has come, to do politics. Back then, against Hitler, they clenched their puny little fists in the trouser pocket of their officer uniforms. The other hand was still only interested in business, profit. They weren't actively involved in the war. Certainly didn't help to ensure our borders were closed to those who couldn't afford to pay first the Reich flight tax and then the people smugglers – I defy anyone to tell me otherwise. Having a different opinion was enough to end up on the list of people who would've been shot first. Want to see it? Get Tat to show you next Sunday. His name was on it. The shoemaker in the next village would've fired the shot. A shoemaker! A shoemaker, whose dream it was to make gents' shoes for the industrialists in St Gallen behind all the embroidery. He was always spineless, him. With those shoes, he'd've been kissing the feet of those predestined to be something, or who already were something. Whatever! Forget it, after all it's all history now, right? Now though, this Schwarzenbach guy's shouting out of every marquee he's invited into that, once again, there are people who have no place here, that they should go, should have to go, and his entourage is making out that anyone who disagrees would be better going too. All this flies in the face of the government's recommendations as well. The entire government. It's all in here.

He waved the newspaper at us, tapped the documents Switzerland had sent out to every household, which my mother was reluctant to read.

– They'll do what they want anyhow.

– I hope so, in this case.

– I've nothing to say on the matter. I can't even go and vote yet. So much for the democracy you're vaunting.

Switzerland doesn't trust just anyone. It picks and chooses. It doesn't trust women, for starters, the Peroxide Blonde had said.

Goulash sauce was dripping from the table, bread lying in the lampshade, pasta smoking on the light bulb. My mother started slowly wiping the wall while my father scratched his head and looked up at the lamp.

– Why are we having *pasta* with the goulash anyhow?

– Because we're out of potatoes.

It was quiet for a while. My mother lit a cigarette and threw her cloth into a corner.

– This democracy can shove it!

– The pasta's nearly burning.

– Then get it back down. Remove the bread from the lampshade while you're at it.

With the chair in one hand, my father climbed onto the table, swept whatever was lying there together with his foot, then got up on the chair.

– Nonetheless, what kind of a country is it when Schwarzenbach and his consorts can play with the people's fears, make money out of their fears? – After a war like that, too!

– As if you'd any experience of it. The shoemaker didn't shoot. Here, nobody shot, no one was shot or went up in the air, nothing went to pot, no one had to get away from here, everyone stayed at home, no one was trapped in their cellars if, indeed, there were any for people to hide in. No one starved to death anywhere, or froze to death, or died of fear.

– Thank God for that! And Tat, Tat was just lucky, more so than Grüninger, you know that as well as I do. Standing there, at Customs, and – by night – moving people and goods across the Rhine, from Austria into Switzerland. That's precisely why I ask what kind of a country is it where people applaud those whose opinions play with fire, those to whom all that matters is stoking the flames, and who even have the cheek to call that freedom?

– We have to keep together.

– Oh yes? What do we have to keep together then? I can gladly tell you: their money. Nothing else. For that, they'll even part with democracy. For that, they'll give democracy a kicking because they don't give a shit about it.

– There are a lot of foreigners, you've got to admit. They'll end up being too much for us.

My father, now very quiet, put his glass down slowly.

– Is that so? Let's hope Schwarzenbach and his lot don't get too much for us. You should know why. Hadn't you to get out of France when Hitler has razing it to the ground – in order, supposedly, to liberate it.

My father swept the broken plate up, then stood up again and threw the shovel and bits of plate at the wall, albeit not the one my mother had just wiped. He screamed that foreign infiltration and idiocy were one and the same, and that he couldn't get his head round one thing – why he'd to listen to such idiocy from a woman who was half-French. She spelt out for him what would happen if our Customs collapsed, and foreign countries all just flooded into Switzerland. As a Frenchwoman, she didn't want that either, as someone who was half-French, she was half-Swiss too after all. And if Italian food ended up being all there was, she'd starve to death with a full plate in front of her – their food's so long, you have to twirl it round your fork. And she'd starve to death anyhow cos there'd be no work for him, wasn't he useless when it came to money? Not to mention all the languages – first the Italians and half of Yugoslavia, a bit of Turkey – then it's the Chinese and before you know it, you're eating ćevapčići with chopsticks.

– And anyhow – with your ration coupons here in Switzerland, it was possible for you to sleep through the Nazis. But pretend I didn't say anything. It's all over now anyway, finally over, and I really do know what I'm talking about. – Foreign infiltration isn't idiocy, but a fact. It's already starting here in the stairwell. You can smell it.

Foreign infiltration, initiative, referendum. Three terms. An *issue.* Not a *matter of opinion:*

– *Conviction,* Eli says.

His sigh is longer than the river we live next to.

Edoardo McKenna
Translating Luigi Pirandello

The Flooer in his Mooth (1923)

Well, Ah thoaght as much. Ye're a quiet man. Did ye miss yer train?

It wis really a matter o seconds, ken. Ah jist gote tae the station, an it left right under ma nose.

Ye could uv chased it!

Ach, Ah know. It wis daft, like. Goodness me, if Ah only hudnae been trauchlet wi aw thae hefty parcels an packages... Ah wis loadit like a cuddy, so Ah was! Wemmin, ye see. They're eyways oan aboot messages, it nivver ends! Wid ye credit it, it took me three hale minutes tae fit the strings of aw thae parcels oan ma fingers efter Ah gote aff the coach. Two parcels oan each finger, that's how Ah endit up.

Ye must uv been quite a sight... Know whit Ah wid uv done in yer place? Ah wid uv left them aw in the coach.

Oh aye! An whit wid ma wife huv said? No tae mention ma daughters, an their friends!

Ye shid uv let them skirl their herts oot! Ah wid uv enjoyed the scene nae end.

Och, ye speak like that 'cause mebbe ye don't really know whit wemmin are like whin they go oan hoaliday!

But of course Ah dae. That's exackly how Ah'm sayin so. They aw pretend they'll no need a thing fur their vacation.

If it wis only that! They even go as far as claimin they're tryin tae save money in the process. Then they land in wan ae these villages in the countryside, an the mair mingin, hackit, an scunnersome the place is, the mair they insist oan comparin it tae their maist fantoosh gear! That's wemmin fur ye, ma dear fella! But 'en again, it's their nature, int'it? They say, "If ye could jist nip intae toon, love, Ah could really dae wi this… an that… An seein as ye're there, an if it disnae boather ye- that's the best part, if it disnae boather ye! – ye could mebbe also get me…" An whin ye tell them, "Ma dear wummin, how oan earth d' ye expeck me tae dae aw these messages in jist three oors?", they go like "Blethers, dear, if ye take a coach…" Ye see, the problem is that as Ah wis only supposed tae be awey fur three oors, Ah left ma keys at hame.

O dear. So whit did ye dae?

Well, Ah left that pile o parcels an packages at the station's left luggage, an Ah went tae an inn fur supper. Then, as Ah wis ey feelin fair crabbit, Ah went tae the theatre. It wis bylin hoat in there. Efter the performance Ah asked masel, whit noo? It's awready twelve a'cloack, an Ah huv tae catch the furst train at four. Gettin a room fur a three-oor dover's no wurth the money. An so Ah came doon tae this café. It's no gonnae close, is it?

No sir, it isnae. So ye left aw thae parcels at the station's left luggage?

How are ye askin? Are they no safe there? Ah kin assure ye they were aw neatly tied up…

Oh, absolutely. It's no that… Aw neatly tied up. Aye. Ah kin jist aboot picture them. Tied up wi that particular ability young shoap assistants huv in wrappin up their merchandise. They're sich dab-hauns at that! They huv these nice large foldit sheets ae pinkish paper that are so polished they're nearly a pleasure tae look at, ye see, they're sae smooth ye'd gledly place yer face against them tae feel their saft caress. They spread wan sheet oan the coonter, an wi easy grace they place the lightly foldit fabric oan it, bang in the middle. Wi the back ae their haun they furst lift wan side ae the sheet, then lower the ither yin oan tap ae it, an wioot missin a beat they gie it anither fold. Like an artistic extra, ken. An 'en they bend the coarners intae triangles, slip their tips beneath, an reach oot fur the string boax. They pull oot jist as much as they need fur the joab, an 'en they tie it intae a knoat so quickly that ye've hardly hud the time tae admire their skills whin they present ye wi the parcel an the noose ready fur yer finger!

Ah kin tell ye must uv paid great attention tae young shoap assistants…

Who, me? Ma man, Ah've spent hale days watchin them. Ah kin staun an oor ootside their shoap windaes, easy, keekin at the steer within. Ah simply furget masel. It nearly feels as if Ah could really turn masel, as Ah wish Ah could, intae thon silky fabric, thon striped denim Ah see yonder. Or even wan ae thae rid or pale blue strings the lassies sell at the haberdasher's, huv ye ivver noticed how they dae it? They measure it against the yaird stick, an 'en they twist it intae the shape of an eight aroon their left thumb an pinkie jist afore they wrap it up… Ah look at the customers as they come oot the shoap haudin their bunnle oan their finger or unner their oxter, an follae them wi ma eyes as far as Ah can. An Ah imagine… dear me, if ye only knew the things Ah imagine. But Ah need tae dae that. Aye, Ah need it.

Ye need it? Ah'm sorry… Whit is it ye need?

Tae use ma imagination tae cling oantae life as a climbin plant clings oantae the bars oan a gate. Tae keep ma imagination busy at aw times, gluin it oantae ither folk's lives. Oh, Ah'm no talkin aboot folk Ah know personally, Ah couldnae dae that. Ye wid hardly believe how much their lives gie me the boak. Naw, Ah'm talkin aboot total strangers. Ma imagination can roam freely wi them. No at random, mind ye, Ah actually rely oan any clue Ah might spot in each an evry wan ae them. Ah, tae think how far an deeply Ah kin dig intae their lives! Ah kin even see their hames, an Ah live in them, Ah breathe them in till Ah can perceive… Know the kinna sooch that lingers in evry hoose? Even in yours or mines. But there we don't feel it, we've grown used tae it, an it's become the very breath o wur lives. D' ye know whit Ah mean? Aye, Ah kin see ye're noddin in agreement…

Of course. Ah mean, Ah'm sure ye must draw an extraordinary pleasure oot ae aw this imagination o yours…

Pleasure? Me?

Well, Ah'd presume…

Pleasure, says he! Tell me, huv ye ivver been tae see a well-known private doacter?

Me? Nivver. Ah'm no ill!

No, no, it's no that. All Ah wantit tae know wis if ye've ivver seen the waitin room where these private doacters huv their patients bide their time afore their turn.

Oh aye, Ah wance hud tae chum wan ae ma doaghters there tae huv her nerves examined.

Ach, Ah'm no wantin tae neb. Whit Ah meant wis, huv ye ivver taken a good look at thae waitin rooms? The dark, aul-fashioned sofas, the paddit chairs that often don't match, the toaty wee airmchairs… It's aw haun-me-doon stuff, dumped there fur the orra patient. The room the doacter has set aside fur his ain faimly an his wife's lady-friends his a far richer an plusher furniture, ken. If ye were tae flit some ae thae chairs tae the room that caters fur the general public they'd probably gie ye a sair eye against the mixter-maxter yins common patients make dae wi. Well, Ah'd like tae ask ye whether ye carefully inspectit the chair ye were sittin oan while ye were waitin there wi yer doaghter.

Actually, Ah cannae say Ah huv.

'Coorse ye huvnae. Ye werenae ill. An the patients themsels often pey them nae heed, taken up as they are wi their troubles. Mony a time they jist sit there loast in their thoaghts an gawk at their finger, as it draws meanin-less signs oan the shiny airm-rest. An 'en, as they croass the room efter their examination, tae think o the effect thae chairs huv oan them, thae sel-same chairs they were sittin oan as they expectit a sentence tae be passed oan their unknown illness! Tae fyn thae chairs occupied by other patients wi their ain hidden ailin, or doucely emty afore the next patient slumps in them… Well, whit were we talkin aboot? Oh, right. The pleasure that comes fae imagination. Goad knows why Ah immediately thoaght o wan ae thae chairs in a doacter's waitin room…

Indeed… If Ah must be hoanest wi ye…

Ye cannae follae me, kin ye? Ach, Ah don't know whit Ah'm sayin masel. The thing aboot it is, the links we create between the sindry images in wur heids are so personal, an are so affectit by oor ain byganes an experiences, that we'd surely no unnerstaun wan anither if we didnae pit the hems oan them whinivver we get crackin. That's how thae links often appear tae make nae sense at aw. But see here, Ah suppose the connection in this case could lie in the follaein question: wid thae chairs huv drawn any pleasure in guessin who the next patient tae sit oan them might be? Whit illness might be rilin them, an where they might be gaun efter their examination? Nane, Ah'd say. An neither dae I. There's so many patients comin through, an thae poor chairs are there simply tae be occupied by them. Ma ain business is pretty much the same. Ah am randomly occupied wi various folk. The noo, fur instance, Ah'm occupied wi yersel. An ye kin take it fae me whin Ah say Ah gain nae pleasure at aw fae yer missin yer train, fae the fack that ye'll huv tae jyne yer faimly oan hoaliday, or fae any other hassle Ah might presume tae be fashin ye.

There's quite a few Ah could name, sir, believe you me!

Be thankful if it's only fasht that ye are. There's worse things, ma mannie, Ah kin assure ye. Ah tellt ye that Ah need tae cling oantae ither folk's lives. But Ah fyn nae comfort, indeed nae interest, in the process. Quite the opposite. Ah need tae feel whit a scunner life is, Ah need to see how daft an dytit it is, so's no tae care a doacken if it's pit tae an end. An that requires thorough proof, ken? Oan an oan, it's a constant exercise. Because, ma dear fella, we don't know whit it is, but we feel it, don't we, like a smoorin knoat in wur throats, this unyieldin drooth fur life we nivver quite manage tae slocken. Oor existence is sich a greedy-gutsie efter itsel that we seldom get tae savour it as we plooter through it. The actual taste lies in wur by-ganes, in the memories that bind us tae life. But bind us tae what, ye might ask? Tae this fashious nonsense, this goamy jookery-paukery, this glaikit dargin? Aye, indeed. Indeed. This life ye consider but a trifle an a boather the noo, an Ah dare say even a real curse... who knows whit taste it'll gain in four, five, ten years... an whit relish ye'll discover in the tears ye're greetin the day... An life, dear Goad, the verra thoaght o losin it... 'specially whin it's jist a matter o days... There! Kin ye see her? Yon sad shadda ae a wummin, aroon yon coarner, d' ye see her? Och, she's coorin doon the noo!

What? Who… who is it?

Ye didnae see her, did ye? She's hidin awey.

A wummin?

Ma wifie.

Heck! Yer lady?

She watches me fae afar. An ye can take ma wurd whin Ah tell ye Ah'd feel like gaun ower an pit the clug oan her. But it'd be nae use. She's like wan ae thae straggly bitches, the mair ye kick them, the mair they tag alang at yer heel. Whit thon wummin is gaun through oan ma accoont ye cannae even begin tae jaloose. She disnae eat onymair, disnae sleep… She jist chases me fae a distance, day an night… She could at least huv the decency tae dust thon bauchle she wears oan her heid, an tae brush her claes… She looks mair like a cloot nor a wummin these days. Her hair's gone helplessly grey oan her temples, an hersel jist thirty-four. The wey she gets up ma nose Ah cannae begin tae tell ye. Whiles Ah get a haud ae her an gie her a right shoogle, an scream intae her face "Ya sumph that ye are!" She jist stauns there an takes it. She merely looks at me wi sich eyes, dear me, such eyes that Ah swear ma fingers fair itch tae thrapple her! She simply waits till Ah've gone some distance tae start follaein me aw ower again. Look! There she is, she's hingin oot fae behind the coarner…

Poor lady!

Whit poor lady?! Ye've nae idea! She'd like me tae bide at hame, d' ye unnerstaun, she'd like me tae sit there aw quiet an still, tae be lovinly an thoroughly looked efter… tae bask in the rooms' tidiness an the furniture's cleanliness, tae sink in the perfect silence that wance reigned in wur hoose, measured by the cloack skelpin awaw in the dinin room… That's whit she'd like me tae dae! Noo Ah ask ye, tae let ye unnerstaun the absurdity, no, the macabre savagery, even, o her request, Ah ask ye if ye deem it possible that the hooses in Avezzano an Messina might uv remained aw calmly lined up as streets an squares, there under the muin, jist the wey the toon coonsil hud planned them, hud they known aboot that stramash ae an earthquake that wis gonnae deck them? Michty me, but the hooses themsels wid uv upped wi their stane an lime, an shot the craw fur dear life! An jist think aboot the inhabitants ae Avezzano an Messina, imagine them as they get undressed an ready tae go tae bed, place their shoes ootside the door, an 'en delight in the fresh whiteness o their newly washed sheets, in the knowledge that in a wheen oors they'd aw be deid. Dis that seem possible tae ye?

But mebbe yer lady...

Please hear me oot! If death, ma man, wis like wan ae thae queer, filthy insecks somebdy might casually discover oan us... Ye'd be takin a dauner doon the street, an suddenly a passer-by wid stoap ye, he'd gingerly stretch oot two fingers, an say: "Ah'm sorry, allow me, pal. Ye've gote death sittin oan ye." An wi thae two fingers o his he wid lift it an chuck it away. It'd be grand, wid it no? But death's no like wan ae thae filthy insecks. An many who walk aboot unvexed an gallus don't realize they huv it oan them, an calmly make plans fur the moarra, an the day efter... Now, ma friend, I... Wid ye care tae come ower here, under this lamp? ... Ah want tae show ye somethin... Here, under this moustache o mines... d' ye see that nice purple lump? Know whit it's cawed? Ah, it his an awffy sweet name, sweeter nor honey. *Epithelioma,* that's whit they cry it. G' oan, say it... Ye'll feel its sweetness oan yer tongue. Ep-ith-ee-lee-oh-mah... Death, ye see. She passed by, she drapped this flooer in ma mooth, an said: "Keep it for me, dear, and I shall be back in eight or ten months' time." Noo ye tell me, kind sir, if Ah could possibly sit aboot at hame wi sich a flooer in ma mooth, like thon wretchit wummin wid want me tae dae. Ah shout at her, "So ye're wantin me tae kiss ye, are ye?" "Aye, gie's a kiss," she says. Ye know what she did last week? She scratched her lip with a preen, an 'en she grabbed ma heid, an she tried tae kiss me. Oan the mooth. She says she wants tae die wi me. She's aff her heid. Ah cannae bide at hame. Ah need tae staun behind shoap-windaes, tae wonder at the shoap assistants' skills. Because, ye see, if ma heid goes emty fur a wee minute, ye unnerstaun, Ah could easily kill aw the life Ah kin fyn in somebdy Ah don't even know... pull oot ma revolver an gie the malky tae somebdy who, say, might uv been unlucky enough tae miss his train jist like you did... No, no, nae need tae be feart, ma man. Ah wis only takin a rise oot ae ye. Ah'd raither dae masel in, if ivver. Anyhow, Ah'll be oan ma wey the noo. But... there are some juicy apricots tae be fun these days... how d' ye eat them? Hale, skin an aw, don't ye? Ye jist huv tae press them sideyways an they burst open like two fleshy lips... Pure dead brilliant, so they are. Please gie yer lady an yer doaghters ma best wishes fur their hoaliday. Ah kin jist aboot see them, aw dressed in white an blue, sittin in the shade oan a nice green meadow... Also, Ah beg ye, dae me a favour whin ye get back tae yer village the moarn's moarn. Ah suppose there must be a wee bit ae a stretch between the train station an the village itsel, an at the brek o day ye'll be able tae foot it. The furst gress bush ye'll fyn near the ditch, please coont its blades fur me. As many blades as ye'll fyn, as many days Ah'll be steyin alive. But please be a sport an fyn me a nice, big bush, will ye? Good night tae you, sir.

Notes on the Contributors

Donald Adamson is a Scottish poet and translator who taught creative writing and translation studies in Finnish Universities. He was co-translator for *How to address the fog: Finnish poems 1978-2002* (Carcanet/Scottish Poetry Library, 2005). He has also translated songs for the Sibelius Academy, Helsinki, and for the world music ensemble Värttinä. His most recent poetry collection is *From Coiled Roots* (Indigo Dreams Publications, 2013).

Madeleine Campbell's research explores the concept of translation as a performative rather than representational act. Her work engages with current themes of identity, exile and migration. She has recently completed her PhD at the University of Glasgow titled "Translating Mohammed Dib: Deleuzean Rhizome or Sufi Errancy?" Her interests include francophone literature, surrealism, and ekphrastic and found poetry. Her translations of poets from the Maghreb have been published in the *Book of North African Literature* by California University Press (eds. Pierre Joris and Habib Tengour, 2012) and in *Scottish Poetry in Translation*.

A C Clarke is a Glasgow-based poet and translator, whose latest collections are *A Natural Curiosity* (New Voices Press, 2011), shortlisted for the 2012 Callum Macdonald Award, and *Fr Meslier's Confession* (Oversteps Books, 2012). She is a member of Scottish PEN and has won several prizes, most recently the 2012 Second Light Long Poem competition, as well as being commended in the 2010 Stephen Spender Poetry Translation Competition. Her work included here is from her complete unpublished translation of the 70 Contrerimes of Paul-Jean Toulet for which Douglas Gifford very kindly advised on the Scots versions.

Georgina Collins is a Lecturer in Translation Studies at the University of Glasgow and also works as a freelance translator. She has won an English PEN award for writing in translation and published the first anthology of Francophone African women's poetry, *The Other Half of History*, featuring her own translations into English. Georgina researches the translation of non-standard language and has published a number of articles on translation, including one for *The Linguist* on Gaelic Renaissance.

Christine De Luca (Pearson) was born and brought up in Shetland. She writes in both English and Shetlandic. She has had five collections of poetry published, most recently *North End of Eden* (Luath Press 2010) and *Dat Trickster Sun* (Mariscat, 2014); and, as well as winning prizes in her native Shetland, won the poetry Prix du Livre Insulaire 2007 in France for a bilingual Selected. She has also had poetry translations published in many languages, and attended festivals both in Scotland and internationally. She develops art and literature projects and writes children's books in Orkney and Shetland. Her first novel, *And Then Forever*, was published by *The Shetland Times* in 2011. Her most recent project is a collaboration with three other Shetlanders, a writer and researcher, a traditional musician and a photographer, to tell the story of one of Shetland's abandoned islands, Havera. She is one of Edinburgh's Shore Poets.

Colin Donati, poet and musician, is author of the collections *Rock is Water, or a History of the Theories of Rain* (Kettillonia, 2003) and *Ancient and Now* (Red Squirrel, 2010). He also edited *Robert McLellan: Playing Scotland's Story* (Luath, 2013), the first major collection of Robert McLellan's dramatic works. He performs his own original songs and settings with cellist Robin Mason under the name Various Moons.

114

From time to time he creates original prints with Edinburgh Printmakers Workshop. The extract from *Crime and Punishment* is from his complete Scots translation of the same.

Morna Fleming is a former secondary school English teacher and current independent scholar originally specializing in the lyric poetry of the court of King James VI and I in Scotland and Great Britain, on which she has published widely, but she now expanding her interest into the cultural context and writings in various forms of the turn of the 17th century. As secretary of the Robert Henryson Society in Dunfermline, Fife, Scotland, she also has a passion for the poetry of one of Scotland's greatest poets and regularly organizes opportunities for academic and popular examination and discussion of his works.

Richie McCaffery is in his third year of a PhD which looks at the Scottish poetry of World War Two. He is a Carnegie scholar at the University of Glasgow, in the Scottish Literature department, where he is also a teaching assistant. His prose has appeared in places such as The Dark Horse and Scottish Literary Review and he has two published pamphlets of poetry, "Spinning Plates" (HappenStance Press, 2012) and "Ballast Flint" (Cromarty Arts Trust, 2013). His first full poetry collection is forthcoming from Nine Arches Press in 2014.

Edoardo McKenna was born and brought up in Italy in a bilingual Scoto-Italian family, and has always cherished both his heritages and had a keen interest in literature, drama, languages, traditional music and local traditions. After obtaining a degree as translator and interpreter from the renowned SSLMIT, University of Trieste, he relocated to Aberdeen five years ago to attend a Master's Degree course in language planning and minority language protection. He is presently in the third year of his PhD at the same university, where he is investigating the standardization of minority languages.

Donal McLaughlin specializes in translating contemporary Swiss fiction. He translated over 100 writers for the *New Swiss Writing* anthologies (2008-11) and is the voice of Urs Widmer in English. *My Father's Book* (Seagull) was shortlisted for the Best Translated Book Award 2013 (USA). Donal also translates Arno Camenisch, Monica Cantieni, Abbas Khider, Pedro Lenz, and Christoph Simon. He frequently interprets for visiting writers at readings and festivals. In 2012, he featured as both an author and translator in *Best European Fiction* (Dalkey Archive). The author of two short story collections, he maintains a website at donalmclaughlin.wordpress.com

Wilson McLeod is Professor of Gaelic at the University of Edinburgh. He has published widely on issues relating to Gaelic development and minority language policy, as well as Gaelic literature from the Middle Ages to the present.

Sarah Paterson is a PhD student in Scottish Literature at the University of Glasgow. Having previously lived in New Zealand all her life, she moved to Scotland with her husband at the start of 2014 on the William Georgetti Scholarship. Prior to this she was a Master's student at the University of Otago in Dunedin, New Zealand where she studied Kathleen Jamie's poetry under Liam McIlvanney, to whom she is indebted for the ideas behind these poems. Her work has appeared in New Zealand publications Critic, Otago Daily Times, Takahe and Deep South, the last of which she was the 2011 editor. Her debut collection, *Follow the Butterflies*, is available online.

Dennis Smith was formerly Curator of Modern Scottish Collections at the National Library of Scotland where he also edited the *Bibliography of Scotland*, subsequently developed into Scottish Bibliographies Online. He compiled the second edition of the *Scotland* volume in ABC-Clio's World Bibliographical Series (Oxford: Clio, 1998) and edited the *Kincardineshire* volume of the Third Statistical Account of Scotland (Edinburgh: Scottish Academic Press, 1988). He has published articles on a variety of topics from library history to the art of Ian Hamilton Finlay, not excluding contemporary Scottish politics.

Anikó Szilágyi is a doctoral candidate and Graduate Teaching Assistant at the University of Glasgow, where she has taught English Literature, Translation Studies, and Academic Writing. Her PhD thesis focuses on contemporary English translations of Hungarian fiction. *Aliz kalandjai Csodaországban*, her Hungarian translation of Lewis Carroll's *Alice's Adventures in Wonderland*, was published in 2013 by Evertype.

Christopher Whyte / Crìsdean MacIlleBhàin's fifth collection, *An Daolag Shìonach*, with new poems from 2004 to 2007 and uncollected poems from 1987 to 1999, was published by the Department of Celtic and Gaelic of the University of Glasgow in October 2013. His translations of Marina Tsvetaeva's lyrical poems from 1918 to 1920 will appear in New York next August as *Moscow in the Plague Year*. He is a full-time writer, living between Venice and Budapest.

Jennifer Williams's first collection of poetry, *Condition of Fire* (Shearsman, 2011), was inspiredby Ovid's *Metamorphoses* and a journey to the Aeolian Islands. Her second collection, *Locust and Marlin*, was published by Shearsman in 2014 and considers the concepts of home and origin. She has been published in journals including the *Edinburgh Review*, *The Wolf*, *Poetry Wales*, *Fulcrum*, and

Stand. Her poetry has been translated into Greek, German and Dutch and she has translated poetry from Russian, Danish, Spanish, French and Greek. She is Programme Manager at the Scottish Poetry Library.

Notes on the Translated Authors

Monica Cantieni was born in 1965 in Thalwil (Switzerland), and currently lives in Wettingen and Vienna. She is head of Multimedia in the Culture department of SRF (Swiss Radio and Television). The author of numerous short stories in magazines and anthologies, she debuted as a writer with *Hieronymus' Kinder* (*Hieronymus' Children*) in 1996. Her second book *Grünschnabel* (2011) was shortlisted for the prestigious Swiss Book Prize and has already been translated into French, Italian, Spanish, Catalan and Hungarian. An English translation – *The Encyclopaedia of Good Reasons* (Seagull) – will follow in 2014. Monica maintains a website at www.monica-cantieni.net.

Fyodor Dostoevsky (1821-81), Russian novelist, essayist and cultural icon, is one of the great figures of nineteenth-century fiction. His benchmark novel, *Crime and Punishment* (Преступлéние и наказáние), was first published in twelve instalments in *The Russian Messenger* (Рýсский вéстник) in 1866.

Brian Johnstone's work has appeared throughout Scotland, in the rest of the UK, North America and Europe. He has published five collections; his latest, *Dry Stone Work*, is forthcoming from Arc (May 2014). He has read at various international poetry festivals from Macedonia to Nicaragua, and at venues across the UK. Later in 2014 his work will be appearing on The Poetry Archive website. For more information on the poet see http://brianjohnstonepoet.co.uk.

Johnstone's poems featured in this volume and Christopher Whyte's translations were originally commissioned for the work *Cothan/Reliquary* (2003), a set of six artist's books by Jean Johnstone. The books of etchings/pen and ink script, in a limited edition of four, are waxed, wrapped in linen and contained in a paper box. They are held in the collections of the National Library of Scotland, the British Library and the library of the University of St Andrews, and can be viewed there on request. For more information see facebook.com/JeanJohnstoneArtistsBooks.

Riina Katajavuori (b. 1968) is from Finland. Her first collection of poems, *Varkaan kirja* (*The Book of a Thief*), appeared in 1992. Since then she has published five collections of poems, *Kuka puhuu* (*Who's Talking*, 1994), *Painoton tila* (*Weightless Space*, 1998), *Koko tarina* (*The Whole Story*, 2001), *Kerttu ja Hannu* (*Gretel and Hansel*, 2007) and *Omakuvat* (*Self-portraits*, 2011). She has written two novels and a collection of short-stories, seven children's storybooks, and has edited a book of writing by new Finnish talent, *Ryhmä 06* (*Group 06*, 2006). She also writes song-lyrics for various Finnish artists and bands. Her poems were published in the Carcanet anthology *Oxford Poets 2013*. Katajavuori studied at The University of Edinburgh in 1991-92, and has translated Scottish poems by Christine De Luca, Lise Sinclair, Robert Alan Jamieson, Edwin Morgan, Gerrie Fellows, Richard Price, and Andrew Greig.

Eeva Kilpi (b. 1928) is a Finnish poet, novelist and essayist. She spent her childhood in Karelia, the part of Finland ceded to the Soviet Union at the end of the Second World War. She taught English during the 1950s, before becoming a full-time writer in 1959. She has been Chair of Finnish PEN, and has received many prizes and state honours. She has recently been nominated for the Nobel Prize in Literature. Kilpi has seen her work as encompassing three main themes: the experience of evacuation from Karelia, human relationships, and nature. Her commitment to the poetic possibilities of everyday language allows her to include so-called high and low

120

elements – bawdy humour and sexual comedy, as well as delicate expressions of love and loss. More than most poets, she deals in irony, not to destroy or mock, but to achieve compassion – a compassion that extends to the absurdities of old age, as in the group of poems included in this volume.

Māori songs: The six songs featured here will all be familiar to those who have lived in New Zealand, particularly those who went through New Zealand schools in recent decades following increased recognition and nurture of the Māori language, which saw all of these introduced as common songs to learn during between th ages of 3 and 13. "Hine e Hine" is a much-loved lullaby, written by a Māori princess at the start of the 20th century. "Te Rauparaha's Haka" is the best-known of New Zealand's many haka, which are ceremonial dances, often associated with warfare or challenges. This haka is one of New Zealand's most recognizable poems thanks to its performance at the start of rugby matches and other sports events. Te Rauparaha was a warrior chief during the 19th century. "Now is the Hour" is a traditional Māori song that was adapted and became popular during both World Wars as a farewell to soldiers. "Pōkarekare Ana" is a hugely popular and well-known New Zealand song, often referred to as New Zealand's unofficial national anthem. Like "Now is the Hour", it is a traditional song which became popular during World War One. "One Day a Taniwha" is a children's song used largely in early childhood education to introduce children to Māori words and pronunciation. It is sung to the tune of "You are My Sunshine". "E Minaka Ana" has become popular much more recently, but is also described as traditional and of uncertain and possibly communal authorship.

Øystein Orten (b. 1962) is a Norwegian writer living in Hareid, Sunnmøre, not far from the art nouveau city of Ålesund. He has a Master's degree in the Humanities from the University of Bergen, and teaches history, language and literature at upper secondary level in Ulsteinvik. In addition to a work of non-fiction based on material from World War II (2009), he has published three collections of poems (most recently *kjensla av at det ikkje regnar andre stader enn her / the feeling that it is not raining anywhere but here*, 2004), short stories (*Sjabervik*, 2011) and three novels (most recently *Rabarbrakrigen / The Rhubarb War*, 2007). His historical novel *Rasmus the Rebel* was published in 2013. In many of his texts the author circles around small coastal communities in the north-west of Norway, exploring themes like history, landscape, identity and belonging.

Luigi Pirandello was born in Agrigento, Sicily, in 1867. A prolific novelist, playwright and short story writer, he was particularly fascinated by the dichotomy between comic sense and humour. Under the influence of Bergson's irrationalism he undertook an endless exploration of the human psyche, which culminated in his novels *The Late Mattia Pascal* (*Il fu Mattia Pascal*, 1904) and *One, No One and One Hundred Thousand* (*Uno, nessuno e centomila*, 1926). He envisaged human existence as constantly torn between fate's haphazard influence and the individual's attempts to counter it by establishing safe, clearly recognizable roles. These recurrent themes, together with those of death and existential malaise, were echoed in both his early plays and the perceptive descriptions of his *Short Stories for a Year* (*Novelle per un anno*, 1922-1937), and found further expression in *Six Characters In Search of an Author* (*Sei personaggi in cerca d'autore*, 1926) and *Tonight We Improvise* (*Questa sera si recita a soggetto*, 1930). He was awarded the Nobel Prize for literature two years before his death in Rome in 1936.

Haris Psarras was born in Athens, Greece, in 1982. He studied law at the University of Athens and the University of Oxford. He holds a PhD in Philosophy of Law from the University of Edinburgh. Haris has published four books of poetry as well as essays and poetry translations. His poetry has been translated into English, French, German, and Romanian.

Aðalsteinn Ásberg Sigurðsson was born in Húsavík, North Iceland, in 1955. After graduating from the Commercial College of Iceland in Reykjavík, he studied Icelandic language, music and acting. In 1977 he made his literary debut with a book of poetry, *Ósánar lendur (Virgin Soil)*. He has since published many books of poetry and poetry translations, one novel and a dozen of children´s books. He has produced many recordings of his lyrics and songs for children and adults and written for both stage and television. His poems have been translated into numerous languages, and he has participated in many literature festivals. From 1998-2006 he was the president of the Writers' Union of Iceland.

Thor Sørheim was born in 1949 in Oslo, Norway, and grew up in Strømmen, a small industrial town near Oslo. He studied Norwegian language and literature, psychology, and religious history at the University of Oslo. Sørheim's background and temperament lead him to write poems that link the sensibilities of rural and urban Norway. He has published eleven volumes of poetry, one novel and one children's book. His latest poetry collections are *Hegrehøyden* (*Heron Height*, 2002), *Jordprofil* (*Profile of Earth*, 2005), *Døden på andre planeter* (*Death on other Planets*, 2010), and *Vintereika* (*Winter Oak*, 2014). From 1983 to 1985 Sørheim was a member of *The Stunt Poets*, a performance group that worked hard to bring poetry off the written page and into official spaces such as stations and the Parliament, even on to milk cartons. In 1986 he was honoured with The Olav Dalgards Prize for the quality of his longstanding contribution to Norwegian letters as a book reviewer. From 1987 to 1991 he was the chairman of the Literary Board of The Norwegian Authors' Union. Since 1988 he has been working as a freelance writer and poet with a yearly grant from the Norwegian government.

Paul-Jean Toulet, poet, novelist, essayist, was born Paul Toulet at Pau in the Béarnais region of France in 1867. He was brought up in France by his aunts, and on leaving school he spent some years in Mauritius, and then Algeria, before returning to his home country.

Between 1898 and 1912 he lived in Paris, frequented the salon of Madame Bulteau, became a friend of Debussy, and published essays, article, individual poems, and fiction. He died of a brain haemorrhage in 1920. He attracted a following among younger poets, who, like him, were in reaction against the Symbolists and sought to return to a simpler and more natural lyric style. The group became known as *Les Fantaisistes*, and influenced Apollinaire, among others. Toulet's collection *Les Contrerimes* (1921) takes its name from the verse form he invented, where alternate lines of a quatrain rhyme but are unequal in syllabic length, thus allowing a greater sense of movement and spontaneity.